John Ford

On Directors Series

John Ford
Martin Scorsese
The Coen Brothers
Stanley Kubrick
Quentin Tarantino

www.booksites.net/mclean

John Ford

Brian Spittles

An imprint of **Pearson Education**

Harlow, England · London · New York · Reading, Massachusetts · San Francisco
Toronto · Don Mills, Ontario · Sydney · Tokyo · Singapore · Hong Kong · Seoul
Taipei · Cape Town · Madrid · Mexico City · Amsterdam · Munich · Paris · Milan

Pearson Education Limited
Edinburgh Gate
Harlow
Essex CM20 2JE

and Associated Companies throughout the world

Visit us on the World Wide Web at:
www.pearsoneduc.com

First published 2002

© Pearson Education Limited 2002

The right of Brian Spittles to be identified as author of
this work has been asserted by the author in accordance with
the Copyright, Designs and Patents Act 1988.

ISBN 0582 42404 6

British Library Cataloguing-in-Publication Data
A catalogue record for this book is available from the British Library

Library of Congress Cataloging-in-Publication Data
Spittles, Brian.
 John Ford / Brian Spittles.
   p. cm. — (On directors)
 Includes bibliographical references and index.
 ISBN 0-582-42404-6 (ppr)
 1. Ford, John, 1894–1973—Criticism and interpretation. I. Title. II. Series.
 PN1998.3.F65 S68 2002
 791.43′0233′092—dc21   2001038007

10 9 8 7 6 5 4 3 2 1
06   05   04   03   02

Typeset in 10/13pt Giovanni Book by 35
Printed and bound in China
SWTC/01

Dedicated to

Alison, Lesley and Maybritt

Contents

Publisher's acknowledgements

We are grateful to the following for permission to reproduce the pictures which appear in this book:

Columbia Tristar Motion Picture Group for *Two Rode Together* © 1961, all rights reserved; Paramount Pictures for *The Sun Shines Bright* © 1953; Twentieth Century Fox Film Corporation for *The Iron Horse* © 1924, *Young Mr Lincoln* © 1939, *The Grapes Of Wrath* © 1940, *How Green Was My Valley* © 1941, *My Darling Clementine* © 1946, all rights reserved; Warner Brothers for *She Wore A Yellow Ribbon* © 1949, *The Searchers* © 1956, *Sergeant Rutledge* © 1960, *Cheyenne Autumn* © 1964, *7 Women* © 1966, all rights reserved.

We would also like to express our thanks to the Wayne Estate for approving the use of stills from *Stagecoach, She Wore a Yellow Ribbon* and *The Searchers,* which include the image of John Wayne.

All pictures kindly provided by the British Film Institute and The Ronald Grant Archive.

Acknowledgements

Of the very many people to whom I owe thanks, the first must be my editor, Alexander Ballinger, for both intellectual encouragement and very practical support. Film studies students, too numerous to name, on various courses, have contributed in many ways. My colleagues on the University of Oxford Diploma in Film Studies, Jim Hillier, Dr Tony Aldgate and Dr Ann Miller also gave invaluable support. Rosie Martin provided translations of French articles not otherwise available in English, and made many useful suggestions regarding analysis of the movies and structure of the book. The Librarian and all the library staff at Rewley House, Oxford, were most helpful, and the book could certainly not have been completed without their pleasant, cheerful and knowledgeable cooperation. The other Brian Spittles pursued and discovered a vast amount of essential video availability, and generously gave superlative technical support beyond praise or mere thanks. Finally, but by no means least, Margaret Wickett was a measurelessly constructive critic and positive thinker.

Selected filmography

1917   *The Tornado* (101 Bison–Universal)

1923   *Cameo Kirby* (William Fox)

1924   *The Iron Horse* (William Fox)

1928   *Four Sons* (William Fox)

1928   *Hangman's House* (William Fox)

1931   *Seas Beneath* (William Fox)

1934   *Judge Priest* (Fox Film)

1935   *The Informer* (RKO Radio)

1939   *Drums Along the Mohawk* (20th Century-Fox)

1939   *Stagecoach* (Walter Wanger–United Artists)

1939   *Young Mr Lincoln* (Cosmopolitan–20th Century-Fox)

1940   *The Grapes of Wrath* (20th Century-Fox)

1940   *The Long Voyage Home* (Argosy Pictures–Wanger–United Artists)

1941   *How Green Was My Valley* (20th Century-Fox)

1942   *The Battle of Midway* (US Navy–20th Century-Fox)

1946   *My Darling Clementine* (20th Century-Fox)

1947   *The Fugitive* (Argosy Pictures–RKO Radio)

1948   *Fort Apache* (Argosy Pictures–RKO Radio)

1949   *She Wore a Yellow Ribbon* (Argosy Pictures–RKO Radio)

1950   *Rio Grande* (Argosy Pictures–Republic)

1952   *The Quiet Man* (Argosy Pictures–Republic)

1953   *The Sun Shines Bright* (Argosy Pictures–Republic)

1956   *The Searchers* (C.V. Whitney Pictures–Warner Bros.)

1960   *Sergeant Rutledge* (Ford Productions–Warner Bros.)

1961   *Two Rode Together* (Ford–Sheptner Productions–Columbia)

1962   *The Man Who Shot Liberty Valance* (Ford Productions–Paramount)

1963   *Donovan's Reef* (Ford Productions–Paramount)

1964   *Cheyenne Autumn* (Ford–Smith Productions–Warner Bros.)

1966   *7 Women* (Ford–Smith Productions–Metro-Goldwyn-Mayer)

Background

John Ford is one of the greatest and most influential of Hollywood's film-makers. He worked in the industry for over half a century, directing about one hundred and forty movies. This time span and output alone make him a monumental figure. But he was also crucial in developing, and extending, Hollywood's traditions. Stylistically Ford was instrumental in experiment-ing with new camera techniques, atmospheric lighting and diverse narrative devices. Thematically, long before it became conventional wisdom, Ford was exploring issues that concern us so deeply today, such as gender, race, the treatment of ethnic minorities and social outcasts, the nature of history, the relationship of myth and reality. For all these reasons John Ford the man and his films reward thought and study, both for the general reader and viewer and the academic student. Ford's pictures express the world in which they were made, and have contributed to making Hollywood what it is today. Popular cinema would be different had John Ford not been a director. This book will illustrate the excitement, importance, influence, creativity, deviousness and complexity of the man and his films.

It is necessary to start with the deviousness and complexity. Was he John Ford, Jack Ford, Sean Aloysius O'Feeney, John Augustine Feeney or John Martin Feeney or O'Fearna? Was he born in Cape Elizabeth, Maine, USA, in 1894 or 1895? Was he the last of eleven or thirteen children borne by his mother? All these names and features of Ford's origin are variously recorded as facts by different commentators. The problem is not simply a pedantic one. Ford was enigmatically complex, creating myths and legends about himself that throw the unwary critic into disarray. His own life revolves around the dictum from *The Man Who Shot Liberty Valance* (1962): 'When the legend becomes fact, print the legend.' Anyone wishing to explore the phenomenon known as John Ford the Director needs to appreciate that contradictions and ambiguity abound. Even one of Ford's greatest critical admirers, Andrew Sarris, observed with reference to the director's attittude to interviewers and interviews: 'we have in response a record of resistance and evasion that would do honour to the most obscurantist modern artist' (Sarris, 1976, p. 15). Lindsay Anderson, a fine director himself who met Ford on five occasions, described him, among other characteristics, as being 'endlessly evasive . . . His technique was brutal, ruthlessly destructive; by lying, by contradicting everything he'd ever said, by effecting not to understand the simplest question, he could reduce one to dispirited impotence' (Anderson, 1999, pp. 9 and 138). That both these men admired Ford and his work, although in different ways – and Anderson eventually became a friend of the director – illustrates just how difficult a streak Ford had in his complex personality.

One admission Ford made of using his much-proclaimed Irishness to fool someone – or was he double-bluffing? – concerned the raising of the finances to make one of his specifically Irish films, and which was filmed in Ireland, *The Quiet Man* (1952). Ford told how he took the head of Republic Pictures, Herbert Yates, to a romantically thatched and whitewashed cottage in Connemara, where, with tears in his eyes, he claimed that it was his birthplace. Yates is reported to have wept with emotion and sentiment too, and made the money available for the film.

Although there is no doubt that Ford at times misled interrogators, and probably enjoyed doing so, he was also assisted on occasions by sloppy research. David Robinson's attempt to subscribe to the romanticism of Ford's Irish heritage, for example, led him to write of the father who 'came to the United States at fifteen to fight in the Civil War (the side, it seems, was immaterial)' (Robinson, 1968, p. 138). But Ford's father was in Ireland, and only eleven years old when the Civil War ended. He arrived in the USA in 1872, by which time the war had been over for seven years. When such a generally reliable source as Robinson allows himself to be sucked into the vortex of mythologizing, it is clear that the rest of us must venture carefully.

An element of Irishness permeates Ford's output, sometimes in the form of overt themes and setting – as in, for example, *The Quiet Man* and the earlier *The Informer* (1935) and *The Plough and the Stars* (1936) – but more often as a feature of characterization introduced more or less extraneously, although on occasions to highlight comedy. An interesting view of Ford's professional Irishness was expressed by Donal Donnelly, who genuinely was born and brought up in Ireland, and lived and worked there, and who acted for Ford. Donnelly commented that Ford never mastered the correct pronunciation of his first name, and that 'I don't think he was intelligent about Ireland. I think he was *sentimental* about Ireland. Just out of date' (Anderson, 1999, p. 229). Again this is a comment from someone who admired and respected Ford despite the misunderstanding of the real Ireland.

Ford's parents were both Irish immigrants, but they do not appear to be of the entirely dispossessed class of many migrants, although Ford at times

perhaps encouraged people to think his background was more impoverished than it really was. He was born when they were living on a 190 acre
farm, for instance, and brought up the son of a saloon owner in Portland,
Maine – a small-businessman with a respected social standing.

Whatever the misconceptions and doubts about his personal history, there
is now a strong consensus about Ford's status as a director. His death in
1973 made front page news in the major US newspapers. Martin Well
typified responses, commenting that during his working life Ford 'became
the virtually undisputed leader among American film directors' (*Washington
Post*, 1 September 1973). He received the New York Film Critics Award four
times. In the UK *The Times* acknowledged that 'Ford was widely recognized
as one of the great poets of the cinema' (3 September 1973). Two years
earlier John Baxter had commented: 'By any standard, John Ford is one of
the greatest directors the cinema has produced' (Baxter, 1971, p. 9). In
France the *Cahiers du Cinéma* group had recognized Ford's importance and
greatness by paying him the compliment of a special edition of the journal
in 1966. Ford's work was admired and respected within the film industry
too. Orson Welles' 1967 comment has often been repeated: 'I like the Old
Masters. By which I mean – John Ford, John Ford, John Ford' (Rosenbaum,
1993, p. 27). Although Ford had a reputation for being abrasive with actors,
he gained admiration from such diverse performers as the Hollywood screen
stars Robert Montgomery and Henry Fonda, who said of Ford, respectively,
that he 'was a genius' and 'a visual kind of poet' (Anderson, 1999, pp. 228,
225); while Mary Astor and James Stewart both considered Ford 'the greatest'
(Astor, 1973, p. 134; Robbins, 1985, p. 105). The industry awarded Ford
a total of six Oscars during his career. In 1971, as a final honour, Ford
received a citation from the Screen Actors Guild for being 'one of the few
giants in motion pictures' (*Washington Post*, 1 September 1973). Appreciation of Ford goes beyond the USA and Europe too. The Japanese director,
Akira Kurosawa, said: 'From the very beginning I respected John Ford. I
have always paid close attention to his films and they've influenced me'
(Richie, 1984, p. 227).

Consensus, of course, implies dissenters – but no director is universally
admired. The ambiguity about Ford's critical reputation concerns the extent
to which his admirers disagree with one another, and the ferocity of their
debates is unlike that concerning other directors. They differ about which
films are great, and which are ordinary; and about the overall tenor of Ford's
career. It either declined into tired tedium during the 1950s and 1960s, or
blossomed into sage maturity. Every theorist, and viewer, has their own subjective response, and everyone ultimately makes judgements on the quality of
films. The critic's true function, however, is to attempt to illuminate the contexts, themes and cinematic modes of expression as objectively as possible.

Ford was always dedicated to film-making. Around the age of eighteen, in 1913, he left the parental home on the northeast coast of the USA for the west coast boom area of Hollywood. His oldest brother Frank had already established himself as a respected director under the name of Francis Ford, and the man now known as John Ford began working for him under the credited name of Jack Ford. In those relatively early days of the Hollywood industry, specialization had not developed, and he undertook many jobs – props man, technical effects, stunts, bit-part acting, assistant director, editing – a learning process that served him well throughout his career.

Although the dozen or so of Ford's films that are now best known, and most studied, date from 1939 – *Stagecoach* – onward, it is salutary to remember that Ford directed his first film – *The Tornado* – as early as 1917 and was almost halfway through his career before directing that epoch-making Western, catapulting John Wayne into stardom in the process. The experience gained in that time informed what some critics consider among the greatest films ever made.

The experience of working quickly, with limited budgets and often the same people also contributed to Ford's prolific output. He made many more films than any other director of comparable status, about a hundred and forty during his career, almost a third of which were made during the silent era. Many of these have subsequently been lost, and knowledge of them exists only in archival form, such as reviews. However, recently copies of some have turned up, unexpectedly, in the Czech Republic, where they had lain untouched for several decades. Ford's silent experience meant that he learnt his craft when – apart from the intertitles and live music provided in the cinema – all the ideas, information and effectiveness of a film had to be conveyed visually, another crucial factor he carried into the later great works. In fact most of his techniques and thematic concerns can be seen in those early pictures. Indeed, Ford is perhaps the Hollywood director who reigns supreme across the silent and sound eras.

Older brother Francis gave Ford his introduction to studio work, and eventually his break into directing. Ford's attitude to Frank was contradictory, displaying both admiration and professional jealousy. The two brothers both became renowned for their picture composition. Indeed, Ford said of himself in 1964 that he thought first as a cameraman thinks. Two years later, several years after Francis' death, Ford declared: 'He was a great cameraman', clearly making the connection between them, and adding: 'there's nothing they're doing today – all these things that are supposed to be so new – that he hadn't done . . . he was the only influence *I* ever had, working in pictures' (Bogdanovich, 1978, p. 40). While it is true that Frank was a powerful, and good, influence, the statement is a typical Fordian reinterpretation of history, ignoring many other important figures in his career. Perhaps part of the misleading nature of the claim stems from the fact that the brothers did not always get on well together in later years, by which time Frank had been entirely eclipsed as a film-maker – not having directed a film after the talkies had come in – and relegated to playing small 'character' roles. It may also reflect some guilt for the jealousy Ford displayed during Frank's lifetime. Frank Baker, bit player and friend of the Fords, recalled:

> *'Everything that John Ford did, I could see the reflection of Frank. Camera angles and different touches. He'd say, "How do you like that?" And I'd say, "I've seen that before," and he'd go as cold as anything . . . He realized that this isn't me. I'm just walking in his [Frank's] footsteps.'*
>
> *(Gallagher, 1986, pp. 11–12)*

It was not until 1923 that the name John Ford, as opposed to Jack, was first credited, for the film *Cameo Kirby*. In the following year Ford made what is perhaps his most prestigious silent, *The Iron Horse*. In many respects the film sets up Ford's recurrent thematic concerns, in particular the making of the embryonic, modern USA.

Ford was always aware of the times in which he lived. Many of the films of the subsequent almost fifty years reflect or refract contemporary concerns. During that period the USA was engaged in three major international wars – the Second World War (1941–5), the Korean War (1950–3), as part of a United Nations force, and the Vietnam War from the early 1960s. The nation also experienced the social turbulence of the 1930s economic Depression and the civil rights agitation that began in earnest in the 1950s and by the later 1960s became bound up with violent university campus unrest and anti-Vietnam War demonstrations. There were fundamental ideological conflicts too, such as the McCarthyite HUAC (House Un-American Activities Committee) anti-communist activities that were most intense between 1947 and 1954, and by the early 1960s the stirrings of contemporary feminism that threatened, and eventually achieved, some radical social and cultural changes.

All of those factors affected Hollywood in general, but there were significant events that specifically changed the film industry too. Technological developments such as the introduction of sound, and later of colour, and widescreen cinemas were clearly important. Less overt, but ultimately more fundamental, changes occurred within the institutional and organizational framework of Hollywood too. The studio system that began in the silent period, and dominated the industry for over thirty years, began to disintegrate in the 1950s and had been transformed entirely by the time Ford directed his last film.

Film historians generally categorize the studio system period as classical Hollywood, and divide the studios into the majors – the 'Big Five' and the 'Little Three' – and 'Poverty Row', with a few independent producers operating within the main framework. The Big Five were Fox (20th Century-Fox from 1935), MGM (Metro-Goldwyn-Mayer), Paramount, RKO Radio Pictures and Warner Bros. The Little Three were Columbia, United Artists and Universal, for whom Ford began his directing career. The latter group did not possess their own cinemas, and so were reliant on the larger companies for the public exhibition of their movies. The Big Five dominated the industry because they were economically vertically integrated concerns, controlling production, distribution and exhibition. Tino Balio has observed that 'By 1930, the motion picture industry had become, in economic terminology, a mature oligopoly' (Balio, 1985, p. 253). A large industry was controlled by relatively few people, creating an oligopoly, a state of limited competition. The Big Five studios decided what films would be produced, their distribution, in which cinemas they would be shown and when. Richard Maltby has argued: 'they controlled access to first-run exhibition, without which no A-feature could hope to be profitable' (Davies and Neve, 1981, p. 35). This affected everyone in the business, from prop-men to audiences, including directors. Mae D. Huettig, for example, has commented: 'The structure of the major companies is important because there is a real and direct connection between the way in which they are set up, the kind of people who run them, and the kind of films produced' (Balio, 1985, p. 294).

Although the system did not reach its maturity until after the development of sound, and the consequent increase in the costs of film-making, Kristin Thompson and David Bordwell have placed the beginnings of classical Hollywood in the decade in which Ford moved to Hollywood:

> *firms formed in the 1910s would be crucial in the industry. Sam, Jack, and Harry Warner moved from exhibiting to distributing, founding Warner Bros. in 1913 . . . William Fox formed the Fox Film Co. in 1914. Three smaller firms that would merge into MGM in 1924 all began during this era.*
> *(Thompson and Bordwell, 1994, p. 70)*

Ford made over thirty films for Universal between 1917 and 1921, a powerful learning process in a comparatively small company where resources were necessarily limited. Ford established himself as a director who could generally be trusted to produce a saleable picture on time and within budget. These were important qualities in Hollywood, but not universally possessed by young film-makers. In 1920, when Ford was still only in his own mid-twenties, he directed *Just Pals* for the Fox corporation. In the following year he signed a long-term contract with Fox that led to another fifty films through the decade. The central importance of the move for Ford's subsequent career was that Fox was a much more dynamic outfit than Universal, destined to emerge ultimately as one of the Big Five. It is extremely unlikely that Universal could have financed something as expensive as *The Iron Horse*, or later as artistically ambitious as *Four Sons* (1928). Indeed, Ford continued to work intermittently for Fox/20th Century-Fox through to the First World War film *What Price Glory?* in 1952.

By that time the studio system that had categorized classical Hollywood was beginning to break down. In 1948 the 'Paramount Decree', as it is usually known, represented a landmark legal decision. In a test case ruling against Paramount the US Supreme Court decreed that the Big Five's control of first-run movie theatres constituted an illegal monopoly, and ordered that exhibition had to be divorced from production and distribution. This undermined the oligopoly of the Big Five, entailing a restructuring of the industry. Although the process was not completed until 1959 its effects began to be felt from the end of the 1940s. In Searle Kochberg's view:

> *divorcement of exhibition from production–distribution marked the end of the studio era. The next few years saw a retrenchment of the majors. They no longer had a guaranteed market for their films and had to compete with independent producers for exhibition slots. The result was that they found their old studio infrastructure too expensive.*
>
> (Nelmes, 1996, p. 22)

Few cinema historians would disagree with this summary in so far as it goes.

It is, however, necessary to take other considerations into account, as Balio has noted: 'The motion picture industry underwent many revolutionary changes during the postwar period, and it may be impossible to separate the impact of the decrees from the shifts in audience demand and the rise of television' (Balio, 1985, p. 404). In 1947 there were a mere 14,000 television sets in use in the USA, only two years later the figure had reached 1 million and by 1960 90 per cent of US homes possessed a set.

There were other factors affecting the movie industry too. Demographic changes occurred for example, and suburbs expanded without cinema provision. Other forms of leisure activities than cinema-going also intervened in the industry's economics. In 1946, when Ford made *My Darling Clementine*, ticket sales in the USA peaked at 82 million a week. This figure began to decline in the following year and by 1966, when Ford directed his last full feature, *7 Women*, ticket sales were only approximately one-quarter of the peak (though this still represented a formidable number of people, and did not include global audiences). While the earlier movie was more immediately popular than the latter, it is still revealing that, despite twenty years of inflation, *My Darling Clementine* grossed about $4.5 million in its first year, while *7 Women* made less than a third of that figure.

Ford had been in the cinema business for over forty years before television attained its peak, and he made few incursions into the newer form. In 1955 he directed two half-hour slots for the television series *Rookie of the Year* and *The Bamboo Cross*, the latter of which Gallagher describes as 'The low point of Ford's career' (Gallagher, 1986, p. 537). Ford's Western *Wagon Master* (1950) formed the basis of the small-screen series *Wagon Train*, for which he contributed one episode in 1960, The Colter Craven Story. Perhaps Ford's most accomplished television piece is *Flashing Spikes* (1962), which, probably not insignificantly, he made with his then current film cinematographer, William H. Clothier. While a television documentary was made about Ford during his lifetime, *The American West of John Ford* (1971), he was quintessentially a man of the cinema.

To some extent, he did utilize the relative freedom of the studio system's gradual disintegration by making more films that were his personal choice, at the same time mixing them with contract pictures too. As early as 1937, during the height of the studio system's mature oligopoly, Ford and the producer Merian C. Cooper set up their own production company, Argosy, with a view to giving the director more freedom than his studio contracts allowed. Initially, the concept did not get off the ground and Ford continued to work mainly for Fox, but two years later *Stagecoach* was to all intents and purposes produced independently by Walter Wanger and released through United Artists. The following year, 1940, *The Long Voyage Home* was a combined creation by Argosy with Wanger and UA again. Ford was then caught up in the Second World War, in which he had an official position as a film-maker. Argosy eventually came into its own in 1947 with production of *The Fugitive*. It made eight other films over the next six years, four in conjunction with RKO Radio, three with Republic and one with MGM. It was eventually dissolved as a company in 1956, although as Scott Eyman observes of Ford's film of that year: 'The Searchers . . . was an Argosy picture in all but name' (Eyman, 1999, p. 452). It was financial complexities – and some alleged sharp practice by Republic's accountants – rather than artistic problems, or actual economic difficulties, that ultimately led to the closure of the project. Ford continued to direct films for various companies rather than becoming involved with any one in particular. In the later stages of his career he was able to exploit his own reputation and the decline of the studio system to make a number of films that have almost an art-house element to them, and which certainly stretched the Western genre beyond the limits of the time. In this category *The Searchers* was succeeded by *Sergeant Rutledge* (1960), *Two Rode Together* (1961), *The Man Who Shot Liberty Valance* and *Cheyenne Autumn* (1964).

It is possible to see these films as expressing Ford's concern with contemporary issues, although typically they do so by refracting aspects of US history. A reflection is a mirror image, and it can be argued that a film such as *The Grapes of Wrath* (1940) reflects its contemporary society by presenting an audience with a mirror image of itself – this is happening today, this is life in the Depression in which we are living. Another approach to these issues is through documentaries, and Ford was an accomplished director in that field too, as can be seen in the very titles of films like *The Battle of Midway* (1942) and *This Is Korea!* (1951), which are concerned with contemporary wars. Almost at the end of his life Ford visited Vietnam during the war, and although he did not direct the documentary *Vietnam! Vietnam!* (1972), he was involved in its production, editing and writing.

A refraction, on the other hand, is a distorted, although not untrue, image. It resembles, as it were, something seen underwater – the image is recognizable but displaced, the rays of perception are bent by their passage through the water. Ford used history as a deflection of the rays of perception: the themes of the later movies mentioned above are relevant to the 1950s and 1960s – interracial conflict, racism, the nature of historical truth and myth – but they are set in the nineteenth century, displaced in time. As such, they work on at least two levels, both as entertainment Westerns and as intellectual explorations of serious present concerns. Ford's persistent refusal to discuss the pictures in terms of the latter interpretation might be interpreted as an illustration of his self-defensive, anti-intellectual, anti-analytical posture. Then again, the consistency with which the themes occur, and are treated, might be taken to confirm their real importance to Ford.

It is often impossible to date precisely the beginning of any social, political or cultural movement. However, it is possible to assert, without devaluing earlier activities, that 1954 – the year before Ford actually shot *The Searchers* – was seminal in the momentum of the US black civil rights movement. In that year the Supreme Court ruled unanimously against public school – in the US definition of that term – segregation in the case of Brown versus the Board of Education. This was by no means the end of segregation; rather it created the impetus for a more vigorous phase in the struggle for civil rights. Its importance stemmed from the source of the verdict, giving legal backing to the moral imperative. The momentum extended beyond segregated education. In 1955 Rosa Parks was fined in Montgomery, Alabama, for refusing to give up her seat on a public transport bus to a white man. The subsequent protest campaign brought into national – indeed, international – prominence the Reverend Martin Luther King, Jr. In the following year, the Supreme Court ruled that transportation segregation laws were unconstitutional. Again, while this did not mark the end of civil rights abuses, it gave a further impetus to the demands for the end of racial discrimination in other areas such as employment and housing. The historian William H. Chafe has written of The South in that period: 'Blacks earned one-third the family income of whites, feudal-style landlords kept them in poverty... If anyone dared to protest, food, lodging, even life, would be snuffed out' (Chafe, 1986, p. 172).

Not surprisingly the issues became more intense during the next decade, when, for example, 200,000 people marched on Washington in August 1963 to protest against the lack of progress in racial integration. King's speech on that occasion expressed a vision of tolerance and peace:

'I still have a dream. It is a dream chiefly rooted in the American dream ... that one day this nation will rise up and live out the true meaning of its creed: "We hold these truths to be self-evident – that all men are created equal."... [one day] the sons of former slaves and the sons of former slave owners will be able to sit together at the table of brotherhood.'

(Oates, 1994, pp. 260–1)

In the event President Kennedy was assassinated a few weeks later, progress proved too slow for many people and non-violent demonstrations had turned to violence by the end of the decade. But it was during this period of the initial momentum that Ford made those films refracting racial tensions, hostilities, misunderstandings and intolerance.

It is not possible to argue specifically how Ford responded to these momentous national events. As Eyman has observed, Ford 'never let anybody know who the real John Ford was. He wanted nothing, *nothing*, known of his thought processes, his motives, goals or inner needs' (Eyman, 1999, p. 20). Nevertheless, no one who was intellectually alive could have been unaware of those events. They affected the general culture of attitudes and perception, and he was, of course, part of, and involved in, that cultural atmosphere. King's 'dream' speech was delivered before Ford went on location with the *Cheyenne Autumn* unit, and it is difficult to argue that a film of that nature – showing Indians rather than Negroes as the dispossessed and disadvantaged race – was not in some way affected by the ideas of equality and reconciliation currently being debated. King's deliberate use of a Lincolnian tone, and his appeal to the roots of the American Dream, would certainly strike a chord with a director so obsessed by US history in general, and the maker of *Young Mr Lincoln* (1939) in particular.

Ford was by no means a feminist, yet the central concern of his last full feature film was a group of women – his only picture to do so. While *7 Women* does not deal with issues of feminism directly, again it can be seen, at least in part, as a response to an emerging new national cultural consciousness about female roles in society. One of the effects of the rise of black consciousness in the late 1950s/early 1960s was to draw attention to other disadvantaged groups. The historian James T. Patterson has observed:

> The rise of protest movements and the counterculture alerted other aggrieved Americans to the potential of group solidarity . . . 'Power' ideologies also helped to promote a revival of organized feminism, which had been quiescent since the 1920s . . . [as] Betty Friedan pointed out in The Feminine Mystique (1963), an influential demand for equal rights.
>
> (Patterson, 1994, p. 445)

It can be argued that Ford, as an intelligent and informed member of his society, and a leading figure in the formal culture of the Hollywood entertainment industry, responded to contemporary events, attitudes and perceptions by displacing – or refracting – them in the way he knew best, through the lens of US history. Whether or not this is seen as a conscious activity on Ford's part, as a natural reaction to a seemingly changing world – and one less attractive to Ford – or as simply an older man's metaphoric dyspepsia, is a matter of interpretation.

His own claim to be merely an entertainer and nothing more seems somewhat disingenuous. Ford's pictures were certainly made to entertain, but his greatest work pushes beyond simple studio requirements. There is something of a European art-house tendency in Ford's best movies, an innovation in techniques and themes. The manner in which he exploited the collapse of the studio system to develop the Western genre has already been touched on, but Ford's artistic ambitions can be seen earlier in his career. The influence of the German director F.W. Murnau was important in the late 1920s when Ford made such untypically Hollywood films as *Four Sons* and *Hangman's House* (1928) (see Chapter 2). Ford's claims to be a *mere* journeyman entertainer can be interpreted as a defence mechanism for his undeclared high-art aspirations. If he made no special claims for his movies he could not be accused of failing to fulfil them.

Ford's was not a transparent personality. He needed close collaborators – an issue explored further in Chapter 1 – and some of his working relationships were extremely creative, but they were also fraught with tensions. Darryl F. Zanuck, for instance, who became head of 20th Century-Fox in 1935, was the producer of some of Ford's most successful films. These included *Young Mr Lincoln*, *The Grapes of Wrath* and *How Green Was My Valley* (1941) – all movies now held in high critical acclaim. They were made in an atmosphere of attrition between Zanuck and Ford. The director resented the producer's attempts at interference, but needed Zanuck's organization and actually respected his judgement on many issues. Zanuck provided Ford with the tools – finance, cast, etc. – to accomplish the main task of filming, but apparently changed the ending of *The Grapes of Wrath*, Ford subsequently claiming his conclusion had Tom Joad disappearing over the hill. In which case Zanuck himself probably directed the final scene between Ma and Pa. Later Zanuck, as editor, is reported to have changed the end of *My Darling Clementine*, the kiss replacing a handshake that Ford had directed. Although Ford did not at all approve of his pictures being tampered with in this kind of way, and hardly liked Zanuck personally, he did appreciate the collaborative value of the relationship.

Ford made John Wayne into a star, and they became personal friends. Yet in order to maintain that friendship the actor had to let the director beat him at cards whenever they played. Ford could not bear to lose. Very proud of his naval status, eventually being awarded the rank of admiral for his participation in the Second World War, Korea and Vietnam, he was scathing about the Duke's failure to enter the armed services despite being younger. Ford often humiliated Wayne on set, and other actors too. During the making of the Second World War movie *They Were Expendable* (1945), for instance, this took the form of making the actor perform a military salute over and over again, emphasizing the point that Wayne had no service experience. The baiting became so bad that Wayne's co-star, Robert Montgomery, intervened to protect his fellow actor from the director's invective. Yet the two men worked together as director and star for twenty-five years. Wayne realized that Ford got the best performances from him, and the director needed the actor's particular qualities. Wayne was phys-ically big and tough-looking, and could act that part, but he also had a physical grace, a way of walking on the balls of his feet that at times gave his characters an almost balletic style of movement. Wayne's most effective vocal cadence was the modulated fall at the end of a sentence. These qualities enabled him, under Ford's specific guidance – he rarely achieved so much with other directors – to express a vulnerability that gave poignancy to the tough-guy image. From *Stagecoach* to *The Man Who Shot Liberty Valance*, Wayne performed the role of the loner who yearned to be part of mainstream society. Despite their abrasive friendship, Ford and Wayne were symbiotically welded.

Wayne's performances in the Cavalry Trilogy exemplify these features of his work with, and for, Ford. In *Rio Grande* (1950), for example, the third movie of that group, Wayne does play the part of a man, Lt. Col. Kirby Yorke, who is nominally part of mainstream society; he is a husband and a father, but he is also a soldier. The importance of family was a crucial Fordian theme, but in that film the conventional family and the concept of the cavalry as a different, but no less valid, family come into conflict. Wayne's performance manages to portray the difficulty and complexity of the choices for Yorke. This can be seen in relation to the problems many families experienced as servicemen returned from the war, sometimes after three or four years' absence. The Cavalry Trilogy allowed Ford to explore contemporary issues of family, duty, warfare, etc. by distancing them in time in the nineteenth century. All these ideas will be explored further.

The exploration of the past, the reality of history, was at the heart of the emergent protest ideologies of the 1950s and early 1960s, and it also appears as a central theme in *The Man Who Shot Liberty Valance*. In that sense the film is simply a product of its time, and might have been made by anyone with any social awareness. The picture's remarkableness lies in the fact that it is a revising of almost a lifetime's work by a film-maker who had been exploring and expressing the mythology and legends of US history for nearly half a century. It is an intellectually brave admission that the past may have diverse interpretations, that history does not consist merely of the good and the bad, the angels and the devils.

The controversies around Ford's work continue, and many of them will be developed and discussed further in the following chapters. Ford was both a man of his times and his own man. He created entertainment, but simultaneously explored complex ideas. He responded to contemporary concerns, but in his own inimitable way. That enigmatic film-maker and critic, Lindsay Anderson, gave a piece of wonderful advice to the student of films, although he frequently failed to follow it himself: 'The function of the critic is to make clear, not to obfuscate; to interpret rather than to judge' (Anderson, 1999, p. 11). Subsequent chapters will attempt to pursue those goals.

1 Ford's film family

John Ford, more than most Hollywood directors, chose as much as possible to work with the same people regularly. This is most evident in the case of actors, who are very public figures. John Wayne, for instance, first appeared for Ford as an extra in *Hangman's House*, and eventually went on to become his main star actor from *Stagecoach* until *Donovan's Reef* (1963). George O'Brien covered a full forty years, from starring in *The Iron Horse* to appearing in *Cheyenne Autumn*. Harry Carey was followed by his son – Harry Jr, also known as Dobe – forging a connection that lasted almost fifty years. A Ford film unit was like a family, with many familiar faces from one production to another. Some of the regulars were in fact family. Brother Francis had character roles in a number of films, right up to *The Sun Shines Bright* (1953) a year before his death. Another brother, Edward O'Fearna, and a brother-in-law, Wingate Smith, were employed by Ford throughout his career, and son-in-law Ken Curtis became a regular performer as actor, and sometimes singer, as in his role as the hapless Charlie McCorry in *The Searchers*.

Like many families the units were not always harmonious. There are many anecdotes of Ford's tyranny and, on occasions, of his coldness, such as his response to Frank Baker's praise of Francis Ford's camera work quoted in the previous chapter. Also, between his initial work with Ford and fame in *Stagecoach*,

> *Ford suddenly refused to talk to [John] Wayne for three years . . . Wayne's sin was making* The Big Trail *with Raoul Walsh. The great silence began then, the kind of exile Ford's actors came to expect when Ford was not recognized as the proper determiner of their careers.*
>
> (Wills, 1999, pp. 68–9)

Although Mary Astor thought 'John Ford's sets . . . always felt "good"' (Astor, 1973, p. 48), James Cagney was clearly uncomfortable on them. His summary of the experience of working for Ford was blunt: 'there is one word that sums up Jack Ford . . . "malice"!' (McCabe, 1998, p. 271).

Nevertheless, many people, not only performers, were willing to work for Ford time and again. Albin Krebs has observed that Ford 'used the same cameramen, assistant directors, costume designers, grips and electricians in picture after picture' (*New York Times*, 1 September 1973), and he did have a reputation for knowing his production crews – which is not a ubiquitous talent among directors. Harry Carey Jr described to Anderson a typical situation on a Ford set:

> '*people weren't all uptight. He was a terrific disciplinarian, but he was never mean to anyone on the crew. He knew every one of their names, and how many children they had, everyone, even up to the guy who swept up the cigar butts. He knew all of them, and he'd never be mean to any of the crew. He'd only be mean to actors – and sometimes the cameraman.*'
>
> *(Anderson, 1999, p. 215)*

Members of a team who know how other people work are able to short-cut some of the processes and lines of communication. This can be very important in a business as complex as film-making, creating efficiency. Ford was, on the whole, a relatively fast operator. In the very early days he could turn out a two-reeler in a week, and even a film as striking as the 129 minutes long *The Grapes of Wrath* was primarily shot in forty-three days – preproduction and editing, of course, have also to be taken into account when working out the exact time it takes to make a picture. Nevertheless, that is quick shooting. A little earlier, for instance, William Wyler – using the same leading man, Henry Fonda – took at least twice as long, from October 1937 until the end of January 1938, to shoot the much shorter *Jezebel* (94 minutes). The efficiency that equates speed with quality might be measured in this case by the fact that *The Grapes of Wrath* won seven Oscar nominations, and was awarded the coveted statuette for Best Director and Best Supporting Actress – Jane Darwell for her role as Ma Joad.

Ford liked working quickly. Generally, he did not, as some directors do, put his actors through repeated rehearsals, preferring instead spontaneity in performance. Run through, set up, shoot was his preferred style – with everyone knowing their job and trusting the other people involved. There were, though, famous arguments with actors. For example, during the filming of Henry Fonda's last role with Ford in *Mister Roberts* (1955), the director lost his temper to such an extent that he actually punched the actor. That quarrel was over broad issues of interpretation. Fonda had been playing the eponymous role in the theatre for seven years and thought Ford's conception of the comedy was wrong:

*'I didn't like the kind of roughhouse humour that Pappy [Ford] was bringing
to it . . . [he] shot it all wrong. He didn't know the timing. He didn't know
where the laughs were and how long to wait for them to die down. He had
them all talking at once, throwing one line in on top of another. When I
said something he just handed me the script and said, "Here, you wanna
direct?" . . . suddenly he rose up out of the chair and threw a big haymaker
at me and POW, hit me right in the jaw. It knocked me over backwards.'*

(Ford, 1998, p. 268)

Adapting a stage play to the screen is always fraught with problems, and
that is especially true of comedy. The audiences are likely to be of a different
make-up, and the theatrical actor can time lines in response to a specific audience's reactions, whereas the film is made cold. If a director leaves a pause
for a laugh that does not arise, the film begins to look pedestrian, although
Fonda's argument that too many jokes quickly choke one another and create
incoherence is also valid. In the event Ford suffered a serious gall-bladder
problem during the course of filming and was replaced by Mervyn LeRoy.

Although this dispute between Ford and Fonda was somewhat extreme in
its outcome, the director was well known for bullying performances from
actors. The instance of the goading of Wayne on the set of *They Were Expendable* has already been mentioned, and during every movie at least one actor,
sometimes several, were subjected to particular humiliation. A case in point
is Harry Carey Jr's first movie, *3 Godfathers* (1948). Throughout the shooting Ford swore at the young actor, kicked him, implied that he was a mas-
turbator and subjected Carey to the physical torment of leaving him for half
an hour in the 100 degree heat of Death Valley. It was a deep-end introduction to acting, physically and emotionally distressing, but it drew a good
performance from an inexperienced player and the two continued to work
together on many other films.

Some directors work by putting their actors through several takes, then
selecting at the editing stage. Ford preferred, when possible – not with-
standing his bullying of actors – to cut in the camera rather than rely on
editing or editors. Although Ford did some of his own editing, that task
became a Hollywood specialism, and in any case he suffered from studio
interference on occasions and would not necessarily trust a picture to other
hands if it could be avoided. Ford became a one-take director whenever he
could – both to get a spontaneous performance and to allow only a minimum of scope to studio editors. Gallagher has argued: 'Many directors shot
fifteen or twenty times more footage than ended up in the picture, whereas
Ford's ratio was about $2\frac{1}{2}$:1' (Gallagher, 1986, pp. 117–18). Randy Roberts
and James S. Olson concur on this matter, observing that Ford 'seldom
needed more than one or two takes. Probably no other major director made

movies that wasted less film or needed less editing' (Roberts and Olson, 1995, p. 155). These factors were made possible partly by his creation of a kind of repertory company. Ford's Stock Company, as it was known, was a strong feature of the way he worked.

Actors, however, are only the public face of films, and generally do not contribute to a picture's creation beyond their own roles. An exception to this was the older Harry Carey's working relationship with Ford, around 1917 to 1919, when the experienced actor was able to teach the young director a good deal about the business. A film, however, is a collaborative venture. Writers, cameramen, producers, composers, designers can all contribute to the overall conception of the work in hand.

As with actors there were writers with whom he preferred to collaborate. A common Hollywood system that emerged during Ford's time was for a writer to create a script for a producer, who passed it on to a director. However, that system had not developed when Ford began directing, and in the early days the credited scenarist was often George Hively. But perhaps the first truly important writer with whom Ford worked was Dudley Nichols, in the early days of the talkies. They worked together, on and off, from *Men Without Women* (1930) through to *The Fugitive*. Some critics find the earlier 1930s films among the least impressive of Ford's achievements, a view reflected in this comment by Gallagher, a not unperceptive viewer: 'The Ford–Nichols movies were characterized by literary pretense, theatrical values, and heavy Germanic stylization' (Gallagher, 1986, p. 465) When Nichols started writing he had only recently arrived in Hollywood from a successful career as a journalist and critic in New York. That experience, and the effect that such films as Murnau's *Nosferatu* (1922) and *Sunrise* (1927) had on Ford (see Chapter 2), helps to explain the look of the first films, and Nichols has been gracious in acknowledging his debt to Ford in the collaboration. Influences were reciprocal, and those circumstances created a good atmosphere for Ford's imagination.

Whatever the shortcomings of their first picture together Nichols provided Ford with challenges and admired the way the director met them during shooting in 1929: 'I told Ford I feared I would imagine and write scenes which could not be photographed. "You write it", he said, "and I'll get it on film." Well, he did' (Anderson, 1999, p. 238). Nichols gave two illustrations of what at the time were daring and imaginative feats:

'They believed long dolly shots could not be made with the sound camera. He did it – one long shot down a whole street, with men carrying microphones on fishpoles overhead . . . Even put the camera in a glass box and took it on a dive on the submarine. It is old hat now. Not then.'

(Anderson, 1999, p. 238)

17

In addition to the technical innovations that Nichols pushed Ford to risk, the pair went on to make several films that became classics for their overall conception and production. *The Informer* was nominated for six Oscars, and actually won four, including Best Director for Ford and Best Screenplay for Nichols. The ground-breaking *Stagecoach* was another product of the Ford–Nichols collaboration. Nichols' summary of working in Hollywood reveals just how good a director Ford was:

> *'I had very unhappy experiences with other directors, who worked by rote, whose minds were vulgar and unimaginative . . . Ford was a great man for a writer to be associated with, and I have nothing but gratitude for the many things I learned from him . . . we formed a fruitful collaboration.'*
> *(Anderson, 1999, pp. 238–41)*

It was precisely the collaboration that stimulated Ford: the fact of the writer understanding that the camera interpreted the page rather than simply recorded it, as the cameras of the 'rote' directors did.

Although Ford was credited as co-writer on some of his pictures he was not a writer in any strict sense. Roberts and Olson have suggested one reason why Ford worked so well with some writers and not so fruitfully with others: 'He regarded scripts as general outlines, not stone tablets. He cut lines, added lines, combined lines' (Roberts and Olson, 1995, p. 154). Mostly he liked to pare scripts down, to keep dialogue to a minimum. The editor, and aspiring director, Robert Parrish recalled Ford's advice to him on directing actors: 'Don't let them talk unless they have something to say' (Parrish, 1976, p. 143). James Stewart praised Ford for being 'visual . . . for never hesitating to discard reams of dialogue if that was what was required to make a picture work' (Dewey, 1998, p. 3).

There are writers who fight that kind of action to the last ditch, creating an uncooperative atmosphere before shooting or on the set. Phoebe and Henry Ephron, for instance, credited with the writing on their one film with Ford – *What Price Glory?* – actually walked out on the production, which is generally thought to be one of Ford's least successful. The argument was not solely about the script – they also reacted against what they saw as Ford's overbearing manner – but the point is that the director needed people who could put up with that. It was those people who became the collaborators, the Stock Company. Those scenarists did not necessarily like Ford's irascibility and unpredictability, but recognized that his attitudes to them and their work were part of the collaborative experience: a creative tension. It stimulated Ford to create some of his best work.

Nichols accepted this. Comparing the published script of *Stagecoach* with the film, Garry Wills has noted: 'Ford made many departures from the script in filming, and the order of some sequences was altered in the editing' (Wills, 1999, p. 330). One example of how Ford changed Nichols' script concerns Ringo's first appearance. The reason he holds up the stage is that his horse has gone lame, and Nichols, following a literal line of thinking, wrote the horse into the shot. Ford, considering the horse a distraction from the crucial initial impact of John Wayne as Ringo, dispensed with it. The dialogue very briefly gives the necessary narrative information, and the literal-minded viewer might ask, what happens to the horse? The answer is it simply doesn't matter. Indeed, if the horse had remained on screen, the question would have become even more insistent. The impact of Wayne/ Ringo and the forward thrust of the narrative carry most cinema audiences beyond such questions.

Nichols helped to induct another writer, Lamar Trotti, into the Ford fraternity. Nichols has described how he undertook to teach Trotti how to write film scripts. For instance, they co-wrote on Ford's vehicles for Will Rogers (sometimes referred to as 'Fox folksies'), such as *Judge Priest* (1934) and *Steamboat Round the Bend* (1935). Trotti's only solo writing credit on a Ford film was *Young Mr Lincoln*, a rather curious fact, since the subject matter was very dear to the director's heart. Ford thought of himself as something of a Lincoln scholar, and yet he made this film with a scenarist who had been hardly more than a secondary collaborator until then.

This is partly explained by the fact that Ford did not, for all his enthusiasm for Lincoln, initiate the idea. The picture's producer, Kenneth Macgowan, revealed that the original idea was solely Trotti's, and on its basis Zanuck, in his capacity as executive, commissioned a scenario. It was only after the completion of the script that Ford was offered the job of directing, which he accepted, according to Macgowan, with only very minor script alterations. Subsequently, however, Ford claimed that he and Trotti had written the script together, in the manner of his normal collaborations. Nichols' later opinion of *Young Mr Lincoln* was that a very successful artistic venture drew more for its merits from Ford than Trotti. Just where the credit mostly lies is not easy to assess, and that is in the nature of film-making. In any event Zanuck also imprinted his judgement on the film as released. Some comedy was removed – Ford was always happy to put in comic situations and characters – along with a less typical scene of whimsical irony when John Wilkes Booth, the president's eventual assassin, walks past the hard-up young Lincoln as he stands outside a theatre, without the price of a ticket. Ford could still suffer from editors as scenarists did from him. The whole episode is a nice illustration of just how collaborative an exercise the making of a film can be.

Ford's working relationship with another important writer, Nunnally Johnson, was also different from the one he enjoyed with Nichols. Johnson wrote scripts for three Ford films: *The Prisoner of Shark Island* (1936); the much-lauded *The Grapes of Wrath*, for which script Johnson received an Oscar nomination; and *Tobacco Road* (1941). Ten years later he explained that none of them were conceived specifically as Ford scenarios, and that they were all submitted in the normal Hollywood manner:

> *'I wrote the scripts without thought of the director to do them and they were offered to him by Zanuck, who selected all the directors for my pictures in those days. All were accepted in the form offered . . . I can't remember that John ever said anything one way or the other about them. Nor can I remember his ever altering or rewriting any of the scripts on the set . . . the pictures he did with me were . . . completely faithful to the script.'*
>
> *(Anderson, 1999, p. 247)*

Indeed, in Johnson's opinion Ford 'can't write. It just runs him nuts . . . he has thoughts and ideas and has never trained himself to put them down on paper' (Frough, 1972, p. 240). For Johnson the collaborative aspect between writer and director was in the realization of the scenes and characters, and he paid fulsome tribute to Ford's construction of scenes, characterization and use of the camera.

In contrast to what might, or might not, have happened with the Trotti solo scenarist credit, and what Johnson categorically insists did occur with his work, Ford enjoyed a relationship with Frank S. Nugent in the 1940s and 1950s that resembled his collaboration with Nichols in the 1930s and 1940s. They worked closely together to produce a fine central caucus of Ford's canonical achievement. *The Fugitive* was the last film Nichols scripted for Ford, and the director's next film, the following year, was *Fort Apache* (1948), which was written, at Ford's special request, by Nugent. As Nugent had been a journalist, and film critic of *The New York Times*, not a Hollywood scriptwriter, the situation was slightly bizarre. It was as though Ford desired to cover the old territory of the Western while simultaneously wanting to make some kind of fresh start.

Nugent's lack of experience made him more malleable than a hard-headed professional like Johnson, while his time spent reviewing films gave him a basic understanding of how they worked. Ford had taken Nichols on as a writer when he was inexperienced too. The director felt more comfortable, perhaps more secure, with people he could mould. Nugent wrote of his experiences of working for Ford that 'some of them are painful to recall' (Anderson, 1999, p. 242). Although this might suggest that Nugent was the recipient of Ford's infamous tyrannical bullying, it is also true that they worked together over a period of fifteen years, collaborating on some of the finest films in the Ford canon. Ultimately, it was an artistically fruitful and happy partnership.

The Searchers (1956). Ethan Edwards (John Wayne).

Nugent's first script was for *Fort Apache*, and he went on to write scenarios for, among other films: *3 Godfathers*, the remake of Ford's own silent *Marked Men* (1919); the sentimental Irish interlude *The Quiet Man*, which received eight Oscar nominations, including one for Nugent's screenplay; the seminal revisionist Westerns *The Searchers* and *Two Rode Together*; the contemporary social critique *The Last Hurrah* (1958). He also had co-writing credits on such important films as *She Wore a Yellow Ribbon* (1949), *Wagon Master* and *Donovan's Reef*. The length of the period of collaboration, along with the range and importance of the films, indicates just how crucial Nugent was to Ford.

Generally, Nugent was tolerant, even respectful, of Ford's interventions, which possibly reflects the fact that the director was to all intents and purposes the writer's patron. Nugent recalled that Ford advised him to start off by mapping out biographies of the characters, even when they were not directly relevant to the narrative. These formed the basis of characterization, avoiding the pitfall of conceiving characters merely as star types – for instance, the John Wayne type. A comparison of the Nugent-created characters Wayne played in such Westerns as *She Wore a Yellow Ribbon* and *The Searchers* alone reveals the diversity; and when the range is broadened to encompass non-Westerns like *The Quiet Man*, it is clear that there is no simple Wayne type.

Ford and Nugent always, according to the latter, worked closely together. Ford's contribution appears to have been mainly in the cutting of dialogue, although he sometimes added to it too. Nugent described Ford as having 'a wonderful ear for dialogue' (Anderson, 1999, p. 244). Nevertheless, there were conflicts. Speaking to Anderson about *Wagon Master*, on which Ford's son Patrick was his co-scenarist, Nugent described how the writers were dissatisfied with Ford's rough treatment of the written material. This was not solely because of the family connection – Ford was not necessarily always the most tolerant of fathers – for Nugent also spoke of his collaboration with Laurence Stallings on *She Wore a Yellow Ribbon* in similar terms. Stallings' solo scenario for one of Ford's personal favourites, *The Sun Shines Bright*, also received vigorous handling by the director.

Johnson's working relationship with Ford clearly differed from either Nichols' or Nugent's experiences, while Trotti's association remains ambiguous. While many other writers figured in the course of such a long and prolific career, these four men were all, in diverse ways, key figures. It cannot be insignificant that the two longest-standing collaborators, Dudley Nichols and Frank Nugent, had also been introduced to screenwriting by Ford himself. There is a strong sense that Ford knew what he wanted, even if, as Johnson thought, he was not capable of writing it himself. It appears that Ford preferred scenarists who would provide him with the basic material for his visual imagination to work on, but be submissive to his will in what he used and how he used it. Nugent summarized Ford's attitude to his own pictures – whether they were good, bad or indifferent in the following way: 'He makes them his own way to suit himself. I'm sure that is the only standard he considers important' (Anderson, 1999, p. 244).

Cinematographers were also vitally crucial for their collaborative contributions to the completed films. Again, Ford liked to work with people he knew and trusted, making them part of the film-set family, his Stock

Company. These included George Schneiderman, Joseph August, Bert Glennon, Gregg Toland, Arthur C. Miller, Winton C. Hoch, Archie Stout and William Clothier. It could be argued that all these contributed something essential to Ford's career despite his reputation for having an exceptional eye for a frame. Whatever the director sees, and however an editor edits it, it is the photographer who realizes the conception on film.

Harry Carey Jr has stated that Ford was less acerbic towards cameramen than he was to actors or writers, and generally Ford was respectful about photographers during interviews. However, the director could assert his authority in no uncertain terms when the mood struck him. Carey tells of Hoch's initiation into the Stock Company family. On location in the Mojave Desert for *3 Godfathers*, Hoch suggested setting up for a particular shot he thought would be appropriate, to which Ford is reported as replying:

'Do you want to go home right now? Who in the name of Christ do you think you are talking to? I mean, Jesus, you're going to lecture me about your pretty goddamned picture postcard shots? Well, we're not having those kind of shots in this picture! And I tell you where the camera goes.'

(Carey, 1994, p. 19)

As an illustration of the contradictions in statements about, and by, Ford, this anecdote might be measured against Ford's claim to Bogdanovich: 'I never had an argument with a photographer' (Bogdanovich, 1978, p. 46). Having established the terms of the relationship, Ford and Hoch collaborated on several films, concluding with the beautifully photographed *The Searchers*, and including *She Wore a Yellow Ribbon* and *The Quiet Man*, for both of which Hoch was awarded the Oscar for Best Achievement in Cinematography. Clearly, the working partnership did not suffer in any way from Ford's insistence on his own role in it.

Ford's attitude to Hoch might have been influenced by his scepticism regarding Technicolor (all Hoch's photography for Ford was in colour). Technicolor began to become fashionable in the 1930s and at the end of that decade Ford made his first film in that format, *Drums Along the Mohawk* (1939). It is possible that Ford was pressured into using Technicolor for commercial reasons, as the picture demonstrates a somewhat careless attitude. For a director who normally paid such assiduous attention to detail to allow Claudette Colbert to appear as a 1770s character in 1930s fashion make-up, for example, is strange, to say the least. Ford was contemptuous of colour, claiming that anyone could photograph in that format, whereas 'black and white is real photography' (Bogdanovich, 1978, p. 74), and he was never completely won over to Technicolor. Even as late as 1962, *The Man Who Shot Liberty Valance* was, suitably, photographed in black and white.

As with the writers, some of the crucial photographer-collaborators worked with Ford, on and off, over a long period of time, while others made a short but intense contribution. Glennon covered the longest period, twenty-four years, from 1936 and The *Prisoner of Shark Island*, to the 1960 *Sergeant Rutledge*, including among his credits the outstanding *Stagecoach* and *Young Mr Lincoln*, as well as, somewhat ironically in the context, a co-credit for *Drums Along the Mohawk*. Schneiderman worked with Ford over a period of fourteen years, mostly in silent pictures, from the 1920 *Just Pals* through to *Steamboat Round the Bend* (1935). His credits included the prestigious pictures *The Iron Horse* and *Four Sons*, both of which contained some remarkable photography. Ford paid his own tribute to Schneiderman in discussing their working relationship: 'I like to have the shadow black and the sunlight white. And I like to put some shadows into the light. We would talk it over . . . We worked together' (Bogdanovich, 1978, p. 46). This implies a quite remarkable collaboration, for the director is asking the almost impossible of the photographer. However, the truth of Ford's words on this occasion is borne out by the results on film. Schneiderman did indeed transform the concept into cinematic reality.

Surprisingly, Schneiderman was not in Ford's own list of the three greatest cameramen with whom he had worked, although the competition to be in such a trio was intense. The three were named as August, Toland and Miller. August was another of the long-serving group, starting with *Lightnin'* (1925) and going through to *They Were Expendable* (1945). His work for Ford included the challenging *Men Without Women*, with its long dolly shot and underwater photography, and *The Informer*. Although August's cinematography was not one of the six categories to receive an Oscar nomination for *The Informer*, it undoubtedly contributed to the overall impact the picture made. Of all Ford's photographers, August was probably the one who most clearly reflects the influence of Murnau in his use of highly stylized stark shots. The world of an earlier Dublin was portrayed as one in which fear and betrayal isolated individuals from one another. Actions are performed against a brooding and threatening background, mostly created in a Hollywood studio (none of it was shot with the benefit of genuine location).

Toland's input was short, from 1940 to 1943, encompassing *The Grapes of Wrath*, *The Long Voyage Home* and the documentary *December 7th* (1942). *The Long Voyage Home* received five Oscar nominations, including one for Toland's superlative cinematography. His work is marked by a mastery of deep focus, allowing the depiction of two planes of action simultaneously, and a chiaroscuro expressionism that brings out strong contrasts between characters, and characters and their situations. These qualities are clearly displayed in a stunning extended shot in which Smitty, trying to jump ship, runs towards a light in the distance. The light creates a halo effect among the dark angular shadows of the dockside. Shooting directly into a light in that manner, while retaining a coherent image of the ever-diminishing figure, is extremely difficult. In this case it expresses both the character's desperation for flight and also the inevitability of failure. The light is both a beacon promising freedom and ultimately a betrayer of his bid to escape as he is captured by a ring of policemen.

Toland's mastery of lighting, particularly the use of light and dark, can also be seen in *The Grapes of Wrath*. Ford was fulsome in his praise of the photography, pointing out that there was

> 'absolutely nothing but nothing to photograph, not one beautiful thing in there – just sheer good photography. I said to him, "Part of it will be in blackness, but let's photograph it. Let's take a chance and do something different." It worked out all right.'
>
> (Bogdanovich, 1978, pp. 76–8)

That blackness expresses the characters' sense of disorientation and alienation, with figures disappearing into, or appearing out of, very deep and disturbing shadows or darkness. Characters who are being treated as sub-human are often photographed in a ghoulish manner with only part of their faces lit. The director creates the set-up for the scene but it is the cinematographer who lights it, who actually realizes the directorial vision.

Miller was the third photographer in Ford's pantheon. They had a short but profound working relationship. Miller had an uncredited input into the river locations of *Young Mr Lincoln* in 1939, but it was not until 1941 that they collaborated fully on *Tobacco Road* and *How Green Was My Valley*. The latter won four Oscars including Best Photography for Miller. Again, the deep blackness of the lighting is a striking feature. The frame plays on the spectator's imagination – it is not only what is seen that creates interest but also what is implied in the darknesses. The viewer is invited, in fact forced, to complete the details. This draws audiences into the picture, making them active participants rather than passive watchers. There is, too, the invigorating experience of seeing what can be created from 'nothing . . . not *one* beautiful thing'. Although there are no 'picture postcard' shots, each frame is expressive. It is the kind of achievement that is realized only when the artists are working in close collaboration and sympathy.

Ford's attitude to cinematography – that it should serve an end, contributing to the film as a whole, rather than functioning simply as a pretty addition – informed his argument with Hoch. Any photographer who did not understand Ford's attitude to the frame would have a difficult time, but those who did comprehend prospered in the collaboration. It also reflected

Ford's scepticism about Technicolor – it was too easy to be pretty without being expressive. William Clothier, who was in the business for over thirty years and photographed a great many films in both formats, concurred with Ford's view of the skills required: 'It's a hell of a lot easier to shoot color [*sic*] than it is to shoot black-and-white; don't ever let anybody tell you different' (Eyman, 1987, p. 136).

Clothier worked with Ford on and off over a period of time. He was second cameraman to Archie Stout on *Fort Apache* and eventually became first man on four of Ford's late films between 1959 and 1964: *The Horse Soldiers* (1959), *Donovan's Reef* and *Cheyenne Autumn* in colour, and *The Man Who Shot Liberty Valance*. While Clothier is among those (although by no means all critics agree) who think Ford was tiring by that time, his regard for the director remained undiminished. In his opinion Ford 'knew more about photography than any man who ever worked in the movies. He was really a genius' (Eyman, 1987, p. 140). Clothier himself was nominated for an Oscar in respect of his work on *Cheyenne Autumn*. Even towards the end of his career Ford was still capable of inspiring a collaborator.

About *The Man Who Shot Liberty Valance* there is a cautionary tale for scholars. Donald Dewey has written categorically of the film: 'the studio insisted that the picture be shot in black-and-white and on its own sound stages to minimize potential losses' (Dewey, 1998, p. 419). However, in reply to Scott Eyman's question 'Whose idea was it to do *Liberty Valance* in black-and-white?' Clothier reportedly answered 'John Ford's. I didn't like the idea; color was becoming more and more necessary, in the studio's eyes, and I liked working in color. He said, "Goddamn it, we're going to do it in black-and-white; it shouldn't be in color"' (Eyman, 1987, p. 136). These accounts, of course, directly contradict one another. While Clothier was actually on the spot, which gives credence to his view, he was speaking twenty-five years after the event and memory is notoriously unreliable. Also, he might have been misquoted by Eyman – though Eyman does have an extremely high reputation for good scholarship stretching over many years. Clothier's view is consistent with Ford's general attitudes to the two formats, and the style does appear to suit the themes of the film. Nevertheless, it can be dangerous to take any one source on face value.

Film-making is a very complex business, and generally done better by people who collaborate, rather than oppose, one another. While Ford some-times exhibited strange ways of collaborating, although more especially with actors than writers, cameramen and others, the results were more often than not reciprocally rewarding. Ford brought out the best in the best of the people he worked with, just as they inspired him to the heights of his achievements. In particular, he extracted performances from actors of a quality no other director achieved. Wayne's career is a case in point – both in range and quality Ford coaxed, coached, and more often bullied, sustained performances from the Duke that are unmatched in the actor's non-Fordian pictures. The same can be said of all Ford's Stock Company actors, and indeed all members of that elite circle. Collaboration was a mutual process from which the Stock Company members – Ford's film family – and their guests, as well as the director himself, benefited.

2 Ford as auteur

The fundamentally collaborative act of film-making and the concept of the director as an auteur, an author with a recognizable personal signature, would appear to be diametrically opposed phenomena. Yet the theory of auteurism has been influential, although by no means universally accepted, for around half a century, half the lifetime of film-making itself.

In fact one of the controversies concerning auteurism is whether it is a theory with different stages of development, or a number of diverse theories that are not necessarily mutually compatible. The initial idea of the director having a signature, in the way that a painter signs a canvas or a writer produces a novel, was expressed in 1948 by Alexandre Astruc. He argued that the cinema had by then clearly developed a long way from its fairground amusement origins, and was 'becoming a means of expression, just as all the arts have been before it, and in particular painting and the novel . . . it is gradually becoming a language . . . a form in which an artist can express his thoughts' (Caughie, 1999, p. 9). Developing the idea of the analogy of novel and film, Astruc introduced the idea 'of *camera-stylo*' (Caughie, 1999, p. 9), the camera as pen.

The specific use of the term auteur dates from 1954. François Truffaut, then a young critic who had yet to become a director, wrote in the journal *Cahiers du Cinéma* of '*la politique des auteurs*' (Caughie, 1999, p. 35). This idea drew on the concept, found in other writing of the period, that the director rather than the writer was the controlling force in film-making.

The fact that up to the 1950s Hollywood directors worked within the constraints of the studio system meant that it was difficult for them to express a sense of their own personality. While Ford did work under these conditions at times, he was also able to exert a degree of individuality, as the development of the Ford Stock Company clearly illustrates. But it is also true that Ford learnt his craft in a production line system, and had to fight to attain, and retain, a measure of independence from the studios.

Auteurism as a concept was still being developed during Ford's working career. One of its a basic tenets is that a director's work as a whole will exhibit recurring themes and a consistency of style. Ford's work is characterized by both these aspects, which, it might be argued, give his films a recognizable and personal signature. History – reality, legend, mythology – is clearly a recurrent concern. All Westerns, by definition of the genre, are historically based. In Ford's case *Young Mr Lincoln* and *The Prisoner of Shark Island* are also period pieces, as is *Drums Along the Mohawk*, set in the US revolutionary period. Although more up to date, the films set in the 1914–18 war and the Irish Troubles of the early 1920s – such as *Seas Beneath* (1931) and *The Informer* – are engaged with aspects of history too. Indeed, his final full feature, *7 Women*, was set in the China of thirty years earlier.

The great Westerns, from *The Iron Horse*, through *Stagecoach* to *Cheyenne Autumn*, all deal with the creation of the modern (1920s to 1960s) USA through an examination of history, myth and legend. Two films of contrasting genres that are superficially very different deal, specifically, with the relationship of past and present, and in terms of individual memory: *How Green Was My Valley* and *The Man Who Shot Liberty Valance*. The former is set in – a rather Californian – Wales and covers the period roughly between 1890 and 1940; while the latter is set in the US West of the nineteenth century over about thirty years. Both pictures, however, are at least in part about economic, social and political changes, the relationship of individuals to society, and to those historical processes, the role of individual memory and perception, historical actuality and interpretation.

One of the themes of *How Green Was My Valley* that resonates with the 1930s Depression is the closure of the works and the miners' strike. Both the father and the chapel deacon, Mr Parry, speak out against socialism, but the minister and the sons see the necessity for united action by the workers. The issues of socialism/communism and their relation to working-class solidarity in the face of economic deprivation and exploitation also emerged in *The Grapes of Wrath*, where the pro-unionists were repressed with savagery by the forces of law and order acting on behalf of capitalism. These issues were not abstract ones in the period. The aspirations of the have-nots and the fears of those who were financially well off were very real, and clearly in conflict with one another.

How Green Was My Valley is somewhat paradoxical – and it is perhaps the complexity in a superficially simple story that characterizes it as a Fordian auteur feature. The picture starts with a voice-over narrator eulogizing memory:

'I'm going from my valley, and this time I shall never return. I'm leaving behind me my fifty years of memory. Strange that the mind will forget so

How Green Was My Valley (1941). Beth Morgan (Sara Allgood) and Gwilym Morgan (Donald Crisp).

much . . . yet leap clear and bright to what happened years ago and long since dead.'

This links with the film's title: 'Was' implies a consideration of the past, while 'Green/Valley' suggests sentimentality, and nostalgia for a better time and place. The opening monologue confirms the end of an era – 'this time I shall never return' – which also indicates a former leaving and coming back, a narrative prolepsis, or hook. Yet many of the memories recounted through the narration are far from pleasant or idealized: family hardship, conflict, emigration, a disastrous marriage, ostracization, death in pit accidents, not to mention the near-death and partial paralysis of the main character, who is subsequently beaten up at school and by the teacher.

Huw Morgan's personal history mirrors that of the valley – it is one of deprivation and decline. After the strike the coal mine cannot employ as many colliers as before, and Huw's voice-over narration explains: 'some learned that never again would there be work for them in their own valley'. This general lesson is emphasized by the emigration of a brother to 'America' because he foresees the collapse of the valley's mining economy. Sixty-year-old Huw is leaving now because 'slag' covers the valley that half a century ago was full of daffodils. While Huw's remembrance of the past, its glorious greenness, is literally valid, the actual conditions of life, as he himself recounts them, were appalling. The gap between *what* is remembered and *how* it is recalled is a factor in the rupture between the facts of history and attitudes to, and beliefs about, them. The character/narrator, Huw does sentimentalize the past/history, but one of the themes of the film is to depict that process and its consequences. Huw's opening monologue expresses the picture's central irony in his question: 'Who shall say what is real and what is not?' The view of the reality of history and the past expressed by Huw is not necessarily that of the director. The gap between the reality of past experiences and memory of them is a recurring Fordian motif, an aspect of his auteurism, his recognizable thematic signature.

Until 1929 the USA had enjoyed probably three hundred years of more or less unbroken economic expansion, spearheading expanding territory, population and world power. It seemed that the nation's historical momentum could not be questioned. However, the great economic crash of 1929 raised serious doubts about the past, present and future. Patterson's analysis summarizes the consensual view:

> *For millions of Americans who suffered through it, the Great Depression was the most numbing experience of their lives . . . It threatened the faith in economic growth and business values that had been at the core . . . It helped cause lasting changes, especially in politics and attitudes toward the government.*
>
> *(Patterson, 1994, p. 183)*

Ford's films, in one way or another, registered the doubts, without altogether forgetting the memory of glory and real achievement.

The recurrence of what might be called the auteurial concern with the relationship of past and present is evident again over twenty years later in *The Man Who Shot Liberty Valance*. Again, the film is largely recounted in flashback with an implicit comparison of then and now, except that in the later picture, 'now' becomes the late nineteenth century, while 'then' is roughly thirty years earlier. Senator Ransom Stoddard is the man responsible for bringing irrigation to the desert. As his wife, Hallie, comments, emphasizing the auteurial antinomies: 'It was once a wilderness, now it's a garden. Aren't you proud?' Ransom has certainly brought cultivation to the desert, as he has also introduced law and order to the previously anarchic Old West. His status, however, originated in a lie – that he was the man who shot Liberty Valance. Five minutes from the end of the film, in a flashback sequence that contains a further time regression, the truth of history is revealed to Ransom by Tom Donophin, the actual killer. Thus, it becomes clear that Ransom has known all along, before gaining political status and power, that his reputation was built upon a lie – and because the information is revealed on screen the audience is also made aware of this fact. The irony is emphasized by the last words in the film, when the train conductor assures Ransom: 'Nothing's too good for the man who shot Liberty Valance!'

The town of Shinbone, and by extension all of the West, has benefited from Ransom's presence in Washington, so living the lie, exploiting the legend rather than acknowledging the truth of history, might be forgiven. There is, however, a personal and private as well as public aspect to the lie. Ransom realizes that by killing Liberty Valance in the manner and at the time he did, Tom both created the conditions for the legend and actually saved Ransom's life. The action is made more poignant because Tom and Ransom were also rivals for the love of Hallie. Ransom's death would have left the way clear for Tom. Donophin's act was one of enormous magnanimity. In killing Liberty he granted life and liberty to Ransom. On the personal level Ransom has to face the historical fact, or at least the implication of the past, that his wife remained in some way in love with Tom. The final shot of Tom's pauper's coffin deliberately focuses on a flowering cactus rose that lies on top of it – earlier in the movie established as a signifier of Tom's love for Hallie – and during the final train journey, Ransom discovers that Hallie had placed it there. On the public level he and the audience appreciate that the true hero of history, the man who actually shot Liberty Valance, died an unknown pauper.

The sombre reality of history, rather than the celebration of myth and legend, is a central aspect of much of Ford's post-Depression work. It forms a vital element in his status as an auteur. There are many other recurring themes too, in addition to the genre antinomies specific to Westerns and identified by Wollen and Kitses, some of which also occur in Ford's Westerns. Individual responsibility, and the relationship of the individual to the group or community, is extremely important, the most vital community being the family. This is complicated somewhat in such films as *Fort*

Apache, She Wore a Yellow Ribbon, Rio Grande and *Sergeant Rutledge*, in which, to some extent, the cavalry itself becomes a surrogate family. Partly related to this, although also of a quite different dimension, is the theme of moral ambiguity, and the complexity of the relationship between motivations and actions, intentions and actual consequences. Journeys are often used by Ford, both literally within narrative and metaphorically or allegorically – such as the journey of moral discovery. *The Man Who Shot Liberty Valance* both starts and ends with a train journey, and the remembrance that forms the main part of the film means that on their return to Washington Ransom Stoddard, and probably Hallie, have been altered by their time in Shinbone.

The auteurists, such as Sarris, also argue that there is a recurring consistency of style in Ford's films. Bordwell, et al., have expressed it in terms of comparative choices: 'Authors are most readily characterized by the recurrence of particular technical devices – Wyler's deep focus, Von Sternberg's cluttered compositions . . . Whereas John Ford might customarily stage an action around a doorway, Sirk might stage it in front of mirrors' (Bordwell, et al., 1985, p. 78). Certainly doorways feature recurrently, and Ford used deep focus too when it provided an appropriate effect.

Perhaps Ford's most famous doorway shots are those that open and close *The Searchers*, but it is a stylistic technique that is recognizably part of his directorial signature and occurs in other films. In *Sergeant Rutledge*, for example, when Mary Beecher is searching the night-time railway station for the station-master, she passes through a darkened room carrying a lantern; from this shot Ford cuts to another dark room, into which a door opens and a gleam of light reveals an apparently hunched figure. Another cut to Mary holding the lantern that is the source of the light. She is framed in the doorway, concerned and hesitating, her pink dress emphasized strongly against the background darkness and the sombre browns of the walls. After a few seconds Mary advances into the room and, thinking Nath is asleep, shakes him, at which he rolls over to reveal an arrow in his heart. Screaming with shock and horror, Mary recoils, and is again framed stationary in the doorway. She then turns and runs away from the camera back through the outer room, yet again framed through two doorways, before turning right to run out of the station. Emerging from the building, she is momentarily framed in the main doorway before a black hand, suddenly appearing from beyond the frame, dramatically clamps across her mouth. The hand belongs to Rutledge, and he is there to save, not threaten, her – a fact, of course, that she is not immediately aware of.

This episode could be shot in many different ways. The use of doorways creates an emphatic focus for the spectator, constructing a frame within the natural restrictions of the camera lens and the cinema screen. In addition to its aesthetic pleasingness, it has a thematic value too. The doorways can be seen as thresholds, both literally, of course, and metaphorically – or psychologically. Mary is moving into a sequence of new worlds within her experience. Each doorway marks a transition into a previously unknown area of life.

The same is true when Lucy enters the room in which her mother is dying in *The Sun Shines Bright*. As the two have been parted for many years, it is a poignant moment, partly signalled by Lucy's confused hesitation in the doorway. The same film also contains a less dramatic, though equally clear, illustration of this aspect of Ford's authorial style. Judge Priest's forlorn entry into the implacable General Fairfield's house, in order to plead tolerance for the granddaughter he refuses to recognize, is mirrored in the film's final shots of Priest. Framed in the doorway of his own house, he takes the salute at the triumphal march past that marks his unexpected re-election as judge. It is the affirmation of an old man's worth, and he is tearfully moved at what is, in effect, a new lease of life. As Priest turns back into his house, he remarks to Jeff Poindexter: 'I gotta take my medicine. I gotta get my heart started.' (The judge's 'medicine' has been used throughout the movie as a euphemism for whiskey.) He is framed, in a receding perspective, walking slowly through two doorways into the heart of his house, a man valued by the community beyond his own expectations.

A variation on this auterist factor in Ford's work is the use of windows as framing and focusing devices, which also thematically emphasize differences between the internal and external worlds. In *Stagecoach*, for example, Lucy Mallory and Hatfield first encounter one another in the doorway of a hotel coffee room. There is no exchange of dialogue, but the characters pause and Hatfield raises his hat and bows in the gentlemanly manner of the period. Cut to a shot inside the coffee room, where Lucy and her friends sit at a window table looking out on to the street. Hatfield is framed quite deliberately in the square of a window pane. He pauses and looks back at Lucy as she asks her companions who he is. The answer – 'Hardly a gentleman . . . a notorious gambler' – identifies him as a potentially unsavoury character for both Lucy and the audience. Nevertheless, their eyes and body language clearly convey some kind of mutual attraction. Just before the stage leaves, Lucy leans out of one of its windows, which frames her, to look at Hatfield, who now occupies a window seat in the saloon. Although engaged in a game of cards, he looks out towards the stage, framed in almost a mirror image in another window pane, and comments: 'An angel in a jungle.' Thus, a relationship is clinched by the speech, the characters' glances and by the precise visual framing.

A similar use of a vehicle's windows occurs in *The Grapes of Wrath*, in which the Joad family are frequently photographed through the windscreen of their truck. The tight framing perhaps signifies both the strength of a family together – it is often Tom driving with Ma and Pa beside him – and, paradoxically, a sense of confinement, of imprisonment. The Joads are victims of an economic system and circumstances they do not understand or have any control over. Each day they encounter a new world of experience. Every day they make some effort to create their own destiny, and every nightfall sees them as imprisoned by circumstances as before. In fact, it is literally the threat of Tom being sent to prison for breaking parole, among other factors, forcing him to strike out alone, that finally breaks up the family bond of Ma, Pa and Tom. Ford's own original ending to the movie was a shot of Tom disappearing over a hill: the constraints of the tight framing had been broken, but only at the cost of losing family unity.

Another auteurist feature of Ford's work is his use of relatively few close-ups. Ford preferred to present characters in a social context or in juxtaposition. An illustration of this is the shot of McCabe and Gary across the river in *Two Rode Together*. Many directors would have intercut close-ups of the two men, partly facing one another, and employed the 180 degree rule, shooting alternately from behind the right shoulder of one character and the left of the other. There are practical advantages to using only one

Two Rode Together (1961). Guthrie McCabe (James Stewart) and Lt. Jim Gary (Richard Widmark).

camera, but there is a greater artistic advantage. By concentrating on a two-shot, in which the actors are seen simultaneously, and facing the camera, a more immediate and subtle series of reactions and responses is created.

There are many examples of such auteurial choices of style in Ford's films. An instance of his very effective use of deep focus can be seen in *How Green Was My Valley*. Again, thwarted love is a theme. Gruffydd and Angharad are in love, but both are impoverished and she marries the rich mine-owner's son. As the bride and groom leave the church to begin their honeymoon, the figure of Gruffydd appears in the background, framed in silhouette against the sky between the branches of a huge tree and the tombstones. The conventional joy of the foreground action and the poignant tragedy in the deep-field frame creates a powerful contrast without the need for intercut close-ups. The fact that Angharad in the foreground is physically oblivious of Gruffydd adds poignancy to the episode. Furthermore, the activity in the foreground is emphasized by the whiteness of Angharad's wedding dress, and in particular by the way in which her veil is blown up into a huge spiral – an effect caused by the deliberate placing of three wind machines, and not a fortuitous act of nature – set against the darkness of the figure in deep focus in the churchyard.

The scenarist, Phillip Dunne recalled that his script had specified a close-up but that Ford refused to shoot one, on the grounds that if he did, some-one would use it. This is an example of how Ford worked as his own editor whenever possible, always endeavouring to determine the final look of a picture. In the event it is clear that a close-up would have distracted from the effectiveness of the deep focus. In another scene Zanuck, the producer, felt that close-ups were needed to augment the long-shot technique Ford had used to show young Huw tentatively walking again after his illness. On this occasion they were filmed later in the studio and inserted. The film displays fine directing, and creative cinematography by Arthur Miller. Although every photographer has their own style, Wills has also noted that as a controlling force, 'it is striking how much Ford gets stylistic uniformity from different cinematographers' (Wills, 1999, p. 100).

One of the photographic features of the post-1927 films is the debt they appear to owe to the influence of the German director F.W. Murnau, who had arrived in Hollywood to make *Sunrise*. Murnau and Ford were mutually complimentary. The latter praised *Sunrise* as one of the great pictures, while Murnau thought the same of *Four Sons*. There were actual connections between *Sunrise* and Ford's operations. The film featured George O'Brien, a Ford actor who had starred in *The Iron Horse*; it was produced by Fox studios, for whom Ford was also working; and the sets used in *Four Sons* were the ones that had been constructed for *Sunrise*. The crucial factor, however, was the style of filming: camera movement, use of actors, editing, lighting, the incorporation of poetic, metaphoric images that enhance mood, theme and characterization. *Hangman's House* was praised at the time by the influential Wilfred Beaton for 'the beauty of the scenes and the wistful quality of the atmosphere' and for the already established Fordian quality of being 'competent enough to avoid sticking in close-ups at each opportunity' (*Film Spectator*, 12 May 1928).

Ford's refusal to make easy use of close-ups is also evident in *Four Sons*, where at moments of emotional intensity, such as when Frau Bernle learns that her sons have been killed, he eschews the conventional close-up of tear-stained face, preferring a dimly lit static character in the mise-en-scène context of a whole room. The result is to emphasize the isolation and destruction of family, for the room should be brightly lit and full of other characters. In order to encapsulate visually the idea of the disjunction of time that any news of death naturally causes, a clock tower is reflected in a river, but from a position looking towards the actual building, so that the image of its face is upside down. When a character (specifically the postman delivering the catastrophic news, illustrating an economy of script control over characters) tosses a coin into the river, the clock face breaks up in circles, further emphasizing visually the theme of disruption, and that time – life – will never be the same again. The journal *Photoplay* awarded *Four Sons* the accolade of the year's best film against such opposition as the sound version of Victor Sjöstrom's *The Wind*, starring Lillian Gish; Raoul Walsh's *Sadie Thompson*, a prestigious version of a Somerset Maugham story starring the Oscar-nominated Gloria Swanson; and Chaplin's *The Circus*.

Ford is also known for having a relatively static camera that restricts movement to within the frame, or allows characters only to move into or out of the frame, rather than moving the camera to accommodate them. Sarris, for instance, has observed of *7 Women* that when Dr Cartwright, having made her self-sacrificing decision to kill Tunga Khan and commit suicide, strides towards the camera, she is 'forcing three people to react to her movement within the same frame. This movement triggers a series of abrupt actions with explosive force' (Sarris, 1976, p. 185). The dramatic moment becomes emphatic through the auteurial style. The dynamism is encapsulated on screen as a continuous process.

Of course, there are the sweeping pans over spectacular landscapes. These are often employed to emphasize the vastness of space against the smallness of the humans who occupy it. A recurring Fordian pan is to maintain characters in a two-shot as they move, so that as they are seen to be moving they also appear to be static within the frame. The testy lovers' tiff between Cohill and Olivia during the cavalry trek across Monument Valley in *She Wore a Yellow Ribbon* is an example that is repeated with other characters in that and other films.

In that film there is a general consistency of movement across the screen too. Most of the movement away from the camera is diagonally from left to right, while much of the movement towards the camera is right to left. Occasionally this is reversed, or there is movement directly across the screen horizontally. The variations are usually employed for dramatic emphasis, as, for instance, in the parallel scenes of the cavalry first crossing the river and later stampeding horses through the Indian camp. Through these devices Ford establishes an auteurial rhythm of cutting and editing – repetition with variation, building a sense of expectation that is mainly fulfilled but sometimes denied, a feature of his directorial signature.

The use of objects in Ford's pictures also provides evidence of his directorial signature. Examples of this occur in *Two Rode Together*, when Marty Purcell plays her brother's music box as a signifier of her self-identification with him. Although actually blameless, she holds herself responsible for his capture by the Comanche, and as compensation for her father's loss of a son prays 'to be . . . a boy'. Earlier illustrations include the way in which the estranged Mrs Yorke expresses her regret as she handles her husband's clothes in *Rio Grande*, and, more darkly, the manner in which Martha Edwards caresses her brother-in-law's coat to suggest her forbidden love for Ethan in *The Searchers*.

It has frequently been noted that John Wayne's final gesture as Ethan is reminiscent of Harry Carey's appearances as Cheyenne Harry in Ford's early silent days. The director's grandson, Dan Ford, is specific about the intention: 'Ethan . . . crosses his arms so that one hand touches the opposite elbow. (The gesture was an old Harry Carey gesture, and Wayne says today that he did it as a private salute to Ollie Carey.)' (Ford, 1998, p. 273). Ford had cast Olive Carey, Harry's widow, as Mrs Jorgensen in *The Searchers*, while her son, Harry Carey Jr, played the part of Brad Jorgensen – so the director was complicit in the gesture too. It marks a line of continuity over forty years of Ford's work. In the same way, the shot of Martin, framed through a doorway, riding up, leaping off his horse and running into the house is reminiscent of Sam approaching the Sims' farm in *Straight Shooting* (1917). Such self-referential motifs display a confident and assured director putting his signature on his work unashamedly.

Other recurrent features in Ford's pictures that enhance the authorial presence are singing, music, dance and comedy. No matter how sombre the tone, some, or all, of these elements are almost sure to appear. There is probably more singing in Ford's Westerns than in any other director's work. There are, for instance, title songs in *She Wore a Yellow Ribbon* and *The Searchers*; while the Sons of the Pioneers perform a whole act in *Rio Grande*, under the guise of entertaining Mrs Yorke; and in *Stagecoach* the cowardly Mexicans desert the beleaguered travellers while they are being entertained, and distracted, by an apparently impromptu cabaret show. Given the fictional Welsh setting of *How Green Was My Valley*, it is not surprising that the miners frequently break into unaccompanied choral singing, even at one point rendering 'God Save the Queen'. In *Young Mr Lincoln* the eponymous hero plays the Jew's harp in order to demonstrate his enjoyment of simple, man-of-the-people pleasures.

Dance is often used to express social cohesion after strife, as in, for instance, *Fort Apache* and *She Wore a Yellow Ribbon*. In *The Grapes of Wrath* dancing demonstrated the resilience in suffering of the dispossessed, and is the moment chosen by the local ruffians to attempt to provoke those people into violence. The dance in *My Darling Clementine* has a similar purpose (commemorating the new church), but it is turned to comic effect when Wyatt Earp partners Clementine in an ungainly parody of grace and rhythm, emphasizing his unsophisticated Old West bearing. Ford also uses disruption at a formal dance to illustrate a lack of social cohesion, as the unseemly scenes in *Two Rode Together* illustrate.

Ford's comedy is often more slapstick in nature, such as the attempt to arrest Sergeant Quincannon in *She Wore a Yellow Ribbon*, or the antics of the recruits trying to mount their horses for the first time in *Fort Apache*, or the saloon-bar brawls in *Donovan's Reef*, where men prove their friendship to one another by breaking chairs over their respective heads. There is also the reappearance of those characters others see as comic albeit, like Earp's dancing, unconscious on their part. Victor McLaglen's various manifestations as Quincannon, archetypal Irish drinker (though McLaglen was not at all Irish) and boon companion, might also fall into that category – though he was slightly more knowing. Buck, the driver in *Stagecoach*, is one such unaware butt of humour, and Charlie McCorry in *The Searchers* another. Indeed, Andy Devine, who played Buck, retained a place in the Stock Company family and was still around over twenty years later when he appeared as the comic sheriff, Link Appleyard, in *The Man Who Shot Liberty Valance*.

If all film appreciation and analysis contains a measure of subjectivity, surely comedy is the most subjective area. Some spectators respond very happily to slapstick, while others find the same scenes intolerable. *The Quiet Man*, with its endless community fights, won awards. On the other hand, William K. Everson thought it 'a permanent failing of Ford's' films to be 'overloaded with typical lowbrow Irish slapstick comedy' (Everson, 1978, p. 256). Whether or not Ford's knock-about comedy is successful depends on one's own response, but it is undoubtedly part of his auteurial signature.

If auteurism is accepted as a critical theory, or theories, Ford seems to fulfil most of the requirements. Anderson wrote disparagingly of the 'diminution of John Ford from artist to *auteur*', posing the dichotomy *'Auteur or Poet?'* (Anderson, 1999, pp. 10, 191). Sarris, on the other hand, as both an auteurist and one of Ford's most fervent enthusiasts, categorizes the director as both auteur and poet, seeing no contradiction between the two terms. Indeed, Sarris specifically described Ford as 'America's cinematic poet laureate' (Sarris, 1976, p. 50). Attitudes vary about the validity of the concept of auteur, and perhaps it is less valuable to argue one theoretical position against another than to use any critical concept as an analytical tool to aid understanding, interpretation and appreciation of the films.

3 Generically challenged

'My name's John Ford. I am a director of Westerns' (Gallagher, 1986, p. 340 ff.). Ford's self-introduction to a meeting of the Directors Guild in October 1950 is possibly his most quoted, or misquoted, statement. Bogdanovich, in his seminal study of Ford, for instance, uses it as a chapter heading in the slightly variant form: 'MY NAME'S JOHN FORD. I MAKE WESTERNS' (Bogdanovich, 1978, p. 6). Tom Milne begins his obituary of the director in 1973 with those words echoing back to 1950, 'My name is John Ford. I make Westerns' (*Observer*, 2 September 1973). Eyman reports it again slightly differently, with Ford being introduced by Joe Mankiewicz and beginning his speech simply: 'I am a director of Westerns' (Eyman, 1999, p. 384). These four examples illustrate three points.

One is certainly to counsel caution when dealing specifically with quotations, perhaps especially where spoken words are concerned. Another is that Ford was here making a statement about himself that was both true and untrue. Third, it is clear that some writers, exemplified by the sub-editor's headline in the Obituary section of the *Observer*, 'Western maker', have taken him literally at his word. These factors have been central to the idea that Ford was generically limited, a mere maker of Westerns – not only restricted in his range, but furthermore engaged in one of the minor genres.

Ford's statement should not be taken at face value, anyway. The situation in which it was made was fraught with political and personal tensions. At the height of the McCarthy HUAC activity, Cecil B. De Mille proposed that all members of the Directors' Guild should take an oath of loyalty – essentially an anti-liberal political statement. The purpose was to isolate anyone suspected of liberal tendencies, while the longer-term implication would have been the possible creation of a blacklist. De Mille attempted to have the liberal Joseph Mankiewicz removed from the presidency of the Guild, and an extremely heated debate ensued for several hours before Ford made his intervention, identifying himself with the phrase in question. Ford's intervention proved crucial, leading to a vote against De Mille.

It is possible only to speculate as to why Ford chose that particular self-identification. He often exhibited a bluff, no-nonsense exterior – possibly, it has been argued earlier, as a self-defence mechanism to deflect potential criticism. In any event, such a posture would have been appropriate for a politically and emotionally charged meeting which included most of Hollywood's leading directors, some of whom certainly had elevated notions of their own self-importance. Ford's intervention was not egoistic; he was looking for a satisfactory and practical outcome. In order to achieve that, perhaps he felt it necessary to undercut purely personal animosities and prejudices, to get back to the basic issue as he saw it – blacklist or relative artistic freedom.

The concept of genre is in itself complex. The word itself stems from *genus*, more commonly thought of as type – a way of defining films: Western, romance, melodrama, historical, musical, etc. However, there is a critical problem in agreeing on a definition. Most Westerns, for instance, are set in the nineteenth century, and are therefore historical, but not in the sense that *Young Mr Lincoln* or *Drums Along the Mohawk* might be categorized. One of the central narrative threads of *The Iron Horse* is the romance between Davy and Miriam, yet it is not a romance or romantic melodrama as, say, the classic *Now Voyager* (Irving Rapper, 1942) ('don't let's ask for the moon. We have the stars!') or *Casablanca* (Michael Curtiz, 1942), with their stories of poignantly doomed, but transcending, love might be defined. There is diegetic music, integral to the narrative, in a number of Ford's Westerns: the Mexicans in *Stagecoach*; the Sons of the Pioneers in *Rio Grande*; Charlie's singing and guitar playing in *The Searchers*; and there are dances in, for example, *My Darling Clementine* and *Fort Apache* – yet none of these would be generically categorized as musicals.

It is partly a matter of emphasis, of course: the presence of music alone does not constitute a musical; the act of kissing does not create a romance. A number of elements enter into genre definition: stars, plot, narrative, setting, style, etc. Which of these more or less familiar elements carries the most weight in any one film? Taking the matter of Ford and stars, for instance, it is clear that John Wayne is known most widely as an actor in Westerns, from the Ringo Kid in *Stagecoach* through to Tom Doniphon in *The Man Who Shot Liberty Valance*, and beyond with other directors. Yet Wayne starred in *The Long Voyage Home* as Ole Olsen, Sean Thornton in *The Quiet Man*, 'Guns' Donovan in *Donovan's Reef* and the early flying ace Frank 'Spig' Wead in the biopic *The Wings of Eagles* (1957), but clearly that does not make any of those movies Westerns.

Earlier genre theory sometimes had a tendency to place films into one specific category, and to argue that a movie within a genre definition was merely repeating a well-known formula. An important development

My Darling Clementine (1946). Wyatt Earp (Henry Fonda) and Clementine Carter (Cathy Downs).

emerged from the recognition of the limitations of such an approach. Steve Neale has argued, against this theoretic position, that genres are 'best understood as *processes*' (Grant, 1997, p. 170). In genre films, audiences may be offered something similar to previous experiences, but the challenge, interest and excitement come from the variation – it is the unpredictable elements, the shifts of perspective, that make, for example, a Ford genre film distinctive.

This is not merely a fight among theorists. The debate arises from attempts to understand complex phenomena with industry-wide ramifications. Genre is one of the ways in which films are conceived and marketed, and therefore one of the factors potential cinema audiences might be influenced by when deciding whether or not to invest in a box-office ticket for a specific film. Genre, then, amid all its other functions and definitions, is the ground upon which film-maker and audience meet; on which negotiation can take place about familiarity, expectation and creation.

Eyman has argued that 'Ford delighted in pretending to be a roughneck' (Eyman, 1999, p. 18), and it is possible – as has been previously suggested – that in identifying himself as a director, or maker, of Westerns he was perhaps playing the bluff, no-nonsense journeyman film-maker. This was

The Grapes of Wrath (1940). Tom Joad (Henry Fonda) flanked by Casey (John Carradine) and Muley (John Qualen).

certainly a role he liked to assume, and which he took on with gusto in Bogdanovich's 1971 film *Directed by John Ford*, perversely attempting to humiliate one of his most enthusiastic and perceptive critics by rudely refusing to answer perfectly reasonable questions. But perhaps Ford was acknowledging a public persona that portrayed him mainly, even if mistakenly, as a director of pictures in the Western genre. His Hollywood career certainly started in that mould. The vast majority of his films up to and including the 1926 *3 Bad Men* were Westerns, and in all around a third of his movies fell into that genre. Certainly, Ford did make more Westerns than films in any other single genre, but it still left two-thirds of his pictures – about eighty, more than most directors make in their entire careers – in different genres.

Of these other genres, Ford will probably be best remembered for the social dramas such *The Grapes of Wrath* and *How Green Was My Valley*. In fact Thomas Schatz categorizes the former as a 'non-genre' film on the basis that it traces

> *the personal and psychological development of a 'central character' or*
> *protagonist. The central characters are not familiar types whom we've seen*
> *before in movies . . . they are unique individuals whom we relate to less in*

terms of previous filmic experience than in terms of our own 'real-world'
experience.

(Schatz, 1981, p. 7)

On the other hand, it might be argued that these factors are Ford's variant on the typical dramas of the 1930s. This difference of emphasis illustrates one of the important facets of genre theory within film studies, for the latter interpretation invites the student back into consideration of the cinematic context, rather than simply treating a film, *The Grapes of Wrath* in this case, as a unique product. Although it is that too, being Ford's individual contribution to, and transformation of, the social drama genre.

The terms drama and melodrama as applied to genre films of the period are more or less synonymous. Social drama as a distinct concept, or a subgenre, was not a popular form. D.W. Griffith's *Broken Blossoms* (1919) might be considered social drama, and King Vidor directed *The Crowd* (1928), *Hallelujah!* (1929) and *Our Daily Bread* (1934) within the genre, but in the Depression years escapism was much more popular than realism. Social issues were presented directly, as opposed to allegorically, but tended to be subsumed into other genres. Gangster films, for example, such as *Public Enemy* (William Wellman, 1931) and *Little Caesar* (Mervyn Le Roy, 1931), acknowledge the existence of social deprivation, but that is not the main point of the films. Chaplin was also aware of serious matters, but he subsumed them into comedy, as in the satires on capitalism and Nazism, *Modern Times* (1936) and *The Great Dictator* (1940). Ford's problem was to synthesize social drama and entertainment, to present a bleak reality in an interesting and cinematically arresting manner.

The power of *The Grapes of Wrath* stems partly from its juxtaposing and fusing of the conventional constituents of the social drama genre – in so far as it existed at the time – with Ford's individual creative vision. The film had a strong starting point in John Steinbeck's novel, published only the previous year (1939). The novel had an immediate impact, being awarded the prestigious Pulitzer Prize in 1940 (Steinbeck was subsequently, in 1962, presented with the highest honour a novelist can receive, the Nobel Prize for Literature). *The Grapes of Wrath* remained his outstanding achievement. The film was launched on the back of the book's success. The speed with which Zanuck bought up the rights, set the experienced Nunnally Johnson to work on the script and Ford on shooting speaks of urgency, of the belief that something very special was in prospect. Indeed, the film was released within a year of the novel's publication. That process was helped by the fact that Steinbeck approved of, indeed praised and admired, the scenario (despite its length, the book had been written in little over a year, another illustration of creative urgency).

Five years earlier *It Happened One Night* (Frank Capra, 1934) had won the four main Oscars – Best Film/Director/Actor/Actress. Although a fine picture in its way, it was pure sentimental escapism, in which the central idea seems to be that being rich makes no one happy, and being poor makes no one miserable. In 1936 Capra again won the Best Director Oscar for *Mr Deeds Goes to Town*, another film that essentially expressed the same sentiment, and sentimentality. These are examples of how Hollywood liked to see the issues of poverty and wealth depicted in the 1930s. In 1939 Zanuck, by no measure a left-wing sympathizer, instructed Johnson to make his draft script bleaker in depicting the poverty suffered by those migrating from the Oklahoma dust bowl to California. Using script conference notes, Eyman has shown how Zanuck, as producer, outlined to his scriptwriter how he saw the Joad family's experience:

> *Their money practically gone . . . driving into town and asking somebody where they should go about finding work . . . The man just looks at them and laughs . . . Their hopefulness and terrible disillusionment. They drive into the Hooverville camp and their hearts drop at the terrible sights. The futility of what has occurred. They just look at each other as the stark truth dawns on them.*
>
> *(Eyman, 1999, p. 215)*

There is no escapism here for an audience, and the way in which Ford filmed it allowed no retreat into sentimentality.

By combining a broad approach to genre and a close reading analysis of a specific sequence, Ford's contribution to the process of developing the genre of social drama is revealed. It is instructive in this context to examine closely how writer and director responded to Zanuck's ideas. About halfway through the film the Joads have crossed the State line into the promised land of California. The truck is out of gas and they are pushing it along a raised road. Suddenly Pa sees a wide expanse of fertile land, and points towards to it crying 'Ma! Grandma! Look!'; the other members of the family join him and there is a chorus of ecstatic appreciation as the audience share, through a high-angled shot, the view across the valley. Cut to Ma as she emerges from the back of the truck – photographed from below, her monolithic, closely framed figure, reflecting the power of the individual, is juxtaposed with the smallness of the group against the sweep of the landscape. She sits on the running-board and the camera angle changes to almost eye level. Cut back to a high-angled shot of the group against the landscape, then again to a low shot of Ma as Tom runs over to her in celebration of their apparent deliverance. Back to eye level as Ma tells Tom, 'Grandma's dead'. The news casts an ironic light on the triumph of arrival, capturing a mood of mingled optimism and sadness, allowing the death to be presented without sentimentality. The absence of conventional background, non-diegetic, music intensifies rather than diminishes the poignancy. The scene ends with a fade of a low-angled two-shot of Ma and Tom, emphasizing their strength and impressiveness. The whole short episode shows a director completely in command of his material, and refusing to take the easy generic path of melo/drama.

In the next scene, the family are pushing the truck into a town's gas station, again following Zanuck's instruction, but in this case the character they talk to is delineated more fully. Rather than just a stock figure, he is individualized into a cop who migrated from the same area as the Joads two years previously. He is friendly, but warns them there is no work and not to stay in town for fear of arrest, but to go on to the camp. The travellers' poverty is projected by the fact that, much to the gas attendant's chagrin, in answer to his 'How many?' Tom replies emphatically, 'One'. The filming here is generally conventional in terms of shooting, editing and lighting, the ordinariness of the filmic conventions and the matter-of-factness of the dialogue and acting styles underlining, by contrast, the desperation of the characters' situation.

The subsequent narrative is told entirely visually with signposts indicating 'CITY LIMIT' and 'TRANSIENT CAMP 2 MILES'. Ford then cuts to a shot of the battered and over-laden truck entering the camp. The screen is roughly split into bright sunshine in the top half, and deep, dark shadows at and just above ground level, expressing both a lingering hope and foreboding. The objective side shot of the truck turning into the camp changes to one in which the vehicle is advancing towards the camera through the contrasting, but natural, light and dark. Again, there is no cumbersome soundtrack music to overplay or sentimentalize the experience. The only sound is the diegetic labouring of the truck's engine, the clanking of its load and the barking of camp dogs.

Ford then displays his particular directorial genius with a 32 second point-of-view shot. Going beyond the conventions of simple melo/drama, entailing flattering lighting and extended close-ups, Ford and Toland shot the sequence through the windscreen of the Joads' truck as it slowly makes its way into the camp, the camera registering the attitudes of the migrants towards the newcomers. They move out of the truck's way reluctantly, tiredly and only from necessity. The detail is closely observed by the slow-moving subjective camera. The spectator is no longer observer, but participant.

A man and a woman, possibly husband and wife, disinterestedly cross the screen from left to right, a gaunt mother stares at the Joads' truck before walking slowly across in front of it from right to left with her children, while two other staring characters are galvanized into the same action as the truck lumbers on. Men bending over a broken-down car with 'FOR SALE' painted on its bonnet look up listlessly. A woman crosses from left to right, and is followed by another, almost defiantly, as the truck labouringly advances. A woman carrying kindling, as though cradling a child, wanders out from the side and seems to confront the truck. A man, again possibly her husband, joins her briefly before they edge out of the way. There is an air of hopeless atrophy. There is no welcome, no kinship of poverty. They all have dispossession in common, but that does not bring them closer to one another, for they are also in competition for anything that might be going.

Ford has produced a remarkable synthesis, for the spectator, of the emotional impact of subjectivity, the immediacy of the experience of deprivation and an objective intellectual understanding of the situation. The spectator experiences, as the Joads do, the hopelessness that pervades the camp and its occupants; but whereas the dispossessed do not fully understand what is happening to them, and why, audiences should. The irony of their triumph in reaching the State of California leading them to this abject state intensifies the 'terrible disillusionment' Zanuck wanted the film to convey. The point-of-view sequence draws the spectator in emotionally, identifying with the Joads' perception; the documentary style of close observation, the starkness of the lighting and photography, all create an objectifying perspective. It is not just the Joad family who are experiencing terrible disillusionment, but a great many people – 'our people', as Tom refers to them repeatedly.

Social drama here almost becomes documentary, but with the fundamental difference that *true* documentary subjects are merely observed, remaining unaware of the observers. In this sequence the transients are only too aware of the observers, the newcomer Joads, and are either indifferent to them and their troubles or actually hostile. The achievement of the filming is to make the observers – both the Joads and the audience – observed while observing. It both invokes and inverts the essentially voyeuristic nature of cinema. Ford presents emotional and factual truths synthesized, utilizing and transcending the conventions of social drama as he found them. In fact, although apparently paradoxically, it was precisely because he was able to work within the framework of the genre that he was able to extend it.

Robert Lapsley and Michael Westlake have written that

Because any system of rules brings with it the possibility of transgression, genre can be seen as providing a field for variation and elaboration of meaning; hence genre is not something that imprisons a director but precisely allows him a freedom.

(Lapsley and Westlake, 1988, p. 107)

Although this was not written specifically about Ford, his best work exemplifies the idea.

Given the way in which Ford utilized elements of documentary style in some of his feature films, it is not surprising that, despite the fact that they have been eclipsed in the popular imagination and memory by the Westerns, Ford had a formidable reputation in the documentary genre. He won the Oscar over two successive years for Best Documentary: first for *The Battle of Midway* (1942) and then in the following year for *December 7th*. The former was shot during the Second World War when Japanese planes were bombing the Pacific Ocean island of Midway, in the general area of Pearl Harbor, Hawaii, in June 1942. US forces were of course defending their positions too, so it was a full-scale military battle. Axel Madsen recorded the director's description of the episode in an interview with Ford about the experience in 1966:

'I wasn't ready and when the attack came I had only an Eyemo – a 16[mm] camera. I filmed, changing the magazines and putting them in my pocket. I was wounded but the film was safe. The images jump a lot because grenades were exploding very close. Now one does that on purpose – shaking the camera while one films battles. For me it was the real thing because the shells were exploding at my feet.'

(Cahiers du Cinéma, *October 1966,*
previously unpublished translation by Rosie Martin)

This is generally accepted as a true account – Ford was wounded during filming, and in 1973 his coffin was draped with the flag from his Midway headquarters. Ford's achievement was remarkable.

December 7th was a different kind of documentary, registering events immediately before, during and after the surprise Japanese attack on the US naval fleet at Pearl Harbor on 7 December 1941 – the event that conclusively took the USA into the Second World War. Unlike *The Battle of Midway*, however, it was made in retrospect, and initially mainly by Gregg Toland. Ford, however, oversaw the project and is accredited as co-director.

Ford was officially in the US navy during the war years and made a number of documentaries in that capacity. The experiences certainly contributed to his subsequent war film, *They Were Expendable*. It should nevertheless be appreciated that Ford had entered the war picture genre much earlier. For instance, the very titles of the 1930s movies *Seas Beneath*, *The Lost Patrol* (1934) and *Submarine Patrol* (1938) indicate their First World War settings and subject matter.

The military connection was important to Ford, and he was very proud of eventually being promoted to the rank of rear admiral. This was partly a consequence of his work during the 1950–3 Korean War, which resulted in the documentary *This Is Korea!*. Later he directed an orientation film for the Defense Department aimed at servicemen about to be sent to Korea, *Korea: Battleground for Liberty* (1959), which was made in the style of a documentary. The peace remained unofficial and uneasy and many US servicemen were retained in the country; this period also marked the beginning of the USA's involvement in Vietnam. Indeed, although he did not direct it, Ford was involved in a documentary made at the height of that war, *Vietnam! Vietnam!*.

It must not be forgotten that Ford also directed numerous melodramas, family dramas, comedies and historical movies. Ultimately, though, he is associated with the Western genre. Paradoxically, the director who made his reputation in that genre, and who subsequently probably did more than anyone else of the period to develop it, spent thirteen creative years (between 1926 and 1939) working entirely in other genres. When Ford did return to the Western it was, of course, with the seminal *Stagecoach*, a movie that provides a fine example of how it is possible for a director to take the rules of a given genre and deliberately break them in order to expand its inherent possibilities.

Genre-specific innovations in the film include the triumph, and endorsement, of practical morality over theoretical ethics. At the conclusion the hero is released from arrest by the sheriff himself without a legal mandate and goes off to start a new life with a former prostitute (while that word is never used, the signification is clear enough, and she is a repentant and redeemed whore, but the Western world is not usually so forgiving). Indeed, it is the very representative of Law, with the help of the disreputable drunken doctor, who sends the couple off, out of the territory, with the ironic exclamation, 'they're saved from the blessings of civilization'. Given that the criminal now under arrest is the former cornerstone of civilization, the thieving bank manager, the movie is morally radical, inverting the normal, conservative genre expectations.

Stagecoach also presents character differently from most Westerns up to that time. Usually, they were one or two character pictures with lots of fill-ins who had no value outside the needs of the plot. In this film, however, all the passengers, and the driver, have delineated personalities. This complicates genre expectations regarding character focus. There is no single, clear audience focus. At the time the movie was made John Wayne was not a star, and although he now seems the natural focal point, as the Ringo Kid is the film's central character, that would not have been so evident to the original audiences, who had to work it out as they went along.

The use of landscape, too, extended genre expectations. This might be expected from the director who made *The Iron Horse*, but that had been fifteen years earlier. Scenic views are an aspect of Westerns, but in *Stagecoach* Monument Valley almost becomes a character in its own right – a feature Ford would develop further in the two following decades. The scenery is not merely scenic, it contributes to the atmosphere and mood of scenes. Lighting is also used creatively. There are typical expansive sun-lit episodes, but the climactic shoot-out occurs in near darkness, the murderous Plummers first appearing to the Kid as gigantic shadows cast on to a building. While this does not actually break a genre rule, it is challenging the spectator's expectations.

Understanding genre is important because of the expectations/rules implied. As Andrew Tudor has observed:

> The notion that someone utilizes a genre suggests something about audience response. It implies that any given film works in a particular way because the audience has certain expectations of the genre. We can meaningfully talk of . . . breaking the rules of a genre only if we know what these rules are . . . rule-breaking has no consequence unless an audience knows as well.
>
> *(Tudor, 1974, p. 143)*

So genre is a point of contact between film-maker and spectator. Tudor links the idea to two of Ford's late movies: 'Two Rode Together . . . Cheyenne Autumn . . . are slightly disconcerting because they break the rules, particularly vis-à-vis the relation between Indian and white man' (ibid., p. 143). This enables Ford to challenge possible audience preconceptions about the Western genre and its conventional ideology up to the early 1960s. This could also be argued of *The Searchers* and *Sergeant Rutledge*.

There is more than one way to disconcert a spectator, and the experience is not always going to be welcomed. Robert Warshow has observed: 'there is also a different way of violating the Western form. This is to yield entirely to its static quality as legend and to the "cinematic" temptations of its landscape, the horse, the quiet men.' In relating this to *Stagecoach* Warshow argues that it has 'this unhappy preoccupation with style', while *My Darling Clementine* 'goes further along the same path, offering indeed a superficial accuracy of historical reconstruction, but so loving in execution as to destroy the outlines of the Western legend, assimilating it to the more sentimental legend of rural America' (Braudy and Cohen, 1999, p. 664). One of the features of the Western genre, though not all Westerns, is the way it allows a synthesis of violence of action and lyricism of photography: Monument Valley is beautiful, the Indian attack is violent (although it is Indians who suffer the consequences of the violence).

This aspect is even stronger when shooting in colour. The bloody violence can be depicted more graphically, the soft sandstone hues of the mountains more lyrically. This is one reason why Ford was so adamant about shooting *The Man Who Shot Liberty Valance* in black and white, despite it being set in a small, semi-rural Western town, when the form was perhaps more associated with film noir, which was almost invariably contemporary and city based. It is a film that precisely questions the true nature of the Western legend and the myths that constitute history. It is anti-lyrical. In the same way, it can be argued that *My Darling Clementine* refuses to subscribe to the sentimental legend of American rurality by having Wyatt Earp ride away from the burgeoning community and possible marriage at the end.

Genres are not in themselves rigid and static. They develop over time, and against Warshow's view of *Stagecoach* might be set that of Sarris: 'in its own time the Ford film was a stunning stylistic revelation' (Sarris, 1976, p. 82). Ford helped to create what the genre became, and then to contribute to its further development and expansion.

Change is necessary because audiences and the nature of ordinary life are not fixed. In arguing the importance of genre study, Patrick Phillips has written:

> *Genres are formal systems for transforming the world in which we actually live into self-contained, coherent and controllable structures of meaning. Genres can thus be considered to function in the way that a language system does – offering a vocabulary and a set of rules which allow us to 'shape' reality.*
>
> (Nelmes, 1996, p. 127)

The application of this to realist genres such as social drama and war, which are directly concerned with issues of more-or-less everyday life, is not too difficult to accept.

It could, however, be true too of genres such as Westerns, which generally deal with life outside the experience of most viewers. Leo Braudy has observed that, paradoxically, the very nature of those genres may make them more effective:

> *The very relaxing of the critical intelligence of the audience, the relief that we need not take decisions . . . allows the genre film to use our expectations against themselves, and, in the process, reveal to us expectations and assumptions that we may never have thought we had. They can potentially criticize the present, because it too automatically* accepts *the standards of the past.*
>
> (Braudy and Cohen, 1999, p. 617)

Since the Western is inevitably set in the past, the violence, prejudice and intolerance that are inherent in much of its action can be metaphorically set against those characteristics as they exist in the present, and may be subscribed to by some members of an audience. The adventure story that forms the framework of *The Searchers* can then be seen to carry a much deeper challenge.

Barry Keith Grant has commented: 'genres have become the contemporary equivalent to tribal ritual and myth for mass-mediated society' (Grant, 1997, p. 117). The Western certainly contains many ritualistic elements, and deals with the mythology of which history consists. At its best it also explores generalized, universal experiences: the psychologies of rivalry and jealousy in *She Wore a Yellow Ribbon* and *The Man Who Shot Liberty Valance*; of command, service and loyalty in *Fort Apache* and *Rio Grande*; of prejudice and intolerance in *The Searchers, Two Rode Together, Sergeant Rutledge* and *Cheyenne Autumn*; all are relevant Fordian illustrations.

It must not be overlooked that Ford worked in many genres, and won his greatest formal acclamation outside Westerns. Nevertheless the first stage of his career was dominated by them, and in the last half of it he dominated the genre. But in any genre the seminal quality of Ford's work is fundamental. Ford used, developed and expanded whatever he touched.

4 The greatest storyteller

Edward Branigan opens his book on narrative comprehension with the assertion, 'Narrative has existed in every known human society' (Branigan, 1998, p. 1). From its beginning film has contributed to the tradition of narrative, the telling of stories, the relating of fictional and real lives. Ford was a master of that process.

Within the academic discipline of film studies the concept of narratology embodies theoretical approaches to storytelling. It helps to distinguish between different aspects of the processes, as Warren Buckland explains: 'The concept of "narrative" refers to what happens or what is depicted ... and "narration" refers to how that narrative is presented' (Buckland, 1998, p. 27). The former consists of those events and action usually referred to as plot. Classical Hollywood narratives were often dominated by chains of cause and effect, one event or action leading logically, or rationally, to another. Ford's films almost always follow a rational linking of events, which is part of their strong credibility, their closeness to the way most spectators expect actions in their own lives to work out. This is true allegorically, rather than literally, of course – few of us have experienced shooting someone, as in a Western or melodrama, for instance. Nevertheless, in a universalized sense it is understood that the disadvantageous effects of a particular act may well stimulate the desire for revenge in everyday life.

When an audience is shown something as apparently inexplicably barbaric as Ethan Edwards shooting out the eyes of a dead Comanche in *The Searchers*, the film's structure enables the spectator to put the action into two contexts. The immediate explanation is that Edwards is expressing his need for revenge; but he is also doing so in the context of the Comanche belief that without eyes the dead soul will never find rest – Ethan thinks of his vengeance as eternal. The information about space/place and time is organized and presented in such a way as to render the inexplicable comprehensible.

In the usual sequence of events in classical Hollywood movies bad actions are ultimately punished in one way or another, and good characters win out in the end. That is why punishments and rewards occur late in the films – the effects stem from the causes. It is an aspect of the ambiguity of *The Searchers* that the theoretical concepts are valid, but the outcome is enigmatic. The data regarding the past experience, emotions and beliefs of characters is organized, but judgement is left unstated. Ethan is the central protagonist, his motives are explained, but the spectator is not encouraged to identify with him and his actions. He acts barbarically, and while audiences are not expected to endorse his attitudes, they are invited to understand them. It is perhaps a more sophisticated response to understand than to judge – although judgement might follow comprehension, representing then a different calibre of moral assessment – and it is a more useful, more humane, trait to take from the cinema into real life. It is typical that Ford is able to rework an established narrative form into a new dimension without losing any of the power of the traditional narrative momentum.

Theorists such as Branigan, Bordwell, Kristin Thompson and Roland Barthes (all referenced in Further Reading and the Bibliography) distinguish technically between plot and story. Plot is the sequence of events as the spectator sees them, whereas story is the chronological order of actions. This distinction is important in relation to the concept of narration – the way the narrative, what is depicted, is expressed in terms of style, method and techniques. In a sequentially straightforward classical Hollywood film, organized chronologically, there is usually a beginning, middle and end, in that order – but that is not always the most effective form of narration.

Ford used the technique commonly known as flashback in some pictures in order to gain the maximum power and dynamic. In *How Green Was My Valley*, for example, the events that are seen provide an ironic contrast to the subjective voice-over commentary. In *The Long Gray Line* (1955) flashback is used to give historical perspective; while in *The Man Who Shot Liberty Valance* the central thematic is ironically revealed through flashback, as the audience is given the information that reveals when the character Ransom Stoddard had become aware of the vital data.

More complexly, in *The Searchers*, Ethan and Marty's epic pursuit of the Comanches is broken about midway through the movie by Martin Pawley's letter to Laurie Jorgensen, the girl who loves him, and to whom Martin considers himself betrothed. This provides data about the past (letter delivery is slow), about the pursuit, and furnishes the audience with insights into Laurie's feelings. That information will be utilized and built on by Ford later at the lead-in to the planned wedding of Laurie and Charlie McCorry. The letter acts as a trigger for three flashback episodes, and also allows the introduction of typical Fordian comedy into what is otherwise a very bleak film. It is the only letter Marty has sent to Laurie during the five years he has been away, so it might have had a level of poignancy, but she is made to read it aloud to her parents and, very inappropriately and comically, to her new and totally unsuitable suitor, Charlie.

The first flashback is an actuality version of what Marty has written about – the comic episode of the gaining of an Indian wife. The scene on screen is a visualization of Marty's written (literary) narrative. The spectator is given a double perspective of events – the ludicrous nature in which 'the wife' was obtained, and Laurie's interpretation of the script (the letter). Because she is in love with Marty, her reaction is to see the incident as tragically affecting her own interests. Comedy and tragedy are juxtaposed.

There are other perspectives too. Ethan, in the flashback, delights in Marty's embarrassment and discomfort, though neither of the men have the least sympathy for the Indian woman. The narrative also shows, through their responses, how little Laurie's father understands her, and how her mother hopes that she will abandon Marty as a lost cause, along with Charlie's crass opportunism as soon as rival Marty appears to have ruled himself out of the marriage stakes. The upshot is that Laurie is poignantly and terribly isolated. In this respect Laurie and the 'Indian wife', Look, might be seen as thematic parallels. In the second flashback Look attempts to sleep next to Marty, only to be kicked down a slope by him, and in the night she decamps. The final flashback shows, among other scenes, Ethan and Marty coming across an Indian village after a cavalry raid, and finding the 'Indian wife' among the dead.

Even this fairly cursory exploration of narration and narrative reveals Ford's, and in this case scenarist Nugent's too, subtlety in handling plot and story. The double time scheme created by the reading of the letter and the visualization of its contents allows diverse perspectives to be created, complicating possible audience responses. The spectator is not encouraged to take the view, attitude or position of any single character.

Ford had already achieved something similar in his earlier collaboration with Johnson on *The Grapes of Wrath*. Muley's exposition to Tom Joad, and the audience, of the pre-narrative events that forced the Joads and other families to leave Oklahoma is also interspersed with flashbacks presenting the information visually. For instance, the visit of the landlord's agent, the bulldozer montage, the second bulldozer incident involving the confrontation with 'Joe Davis' boy' and the demolition of the Muley family home are all played out dramatically to underpin Muley's monologue. The visualization of the brutality of these scenes helps to explicate Muley's strange, somewhat deranged, state of mind.

The main issue appears to be that no one is to blame. The landlord is being harassed by the banker, who in turn is under pressure from larger financial forces. Muley's insistent question 'Who do we shoot?' cannot be answered. When he threatens the bulldozer's driver it turns out that he is a local man forced to do the job because it is the only work available, and that shooting him would be pointless. Actually showing the scenes, as well as recounting them through narrative, creates a greater dramatic impact and momentum, emphasizing the hopelessness of the sharecroppers' situation. Johnson's powerful, albeit over wordy, script is given visual intensity and immediacy by the flashback sequences.

Ford's preference was for visual narrative. Where verbal information is necessary it is usually brief, exemplified in the report of threatened hostile Indian activity that begins *Stagecoach*. *Fort Apache* starts with a montage sequence behind the credits that clearly relates visually the essence of both narrative and narration. *Rio Grande* opens with a four minute montage sequence before the first expository dialogue – a long time for a classical Hollywood movie – yet everything that is presented visually contributes to the narrative: showing the river, the southwest landscape, the army cavalry patrol returning to its fort, excited children, apprehensive women, the

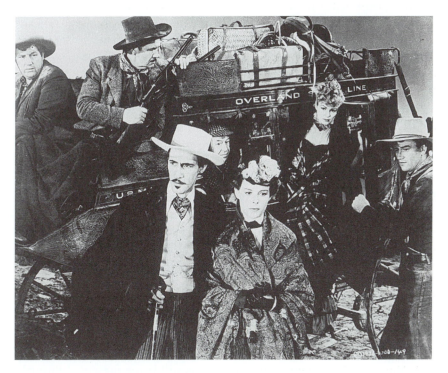

Stagecoach (1939). From left to right: Buck (Andy Devine), Sheriff Curly Willcox (George Bancroft), Hatfield (John Carradine), Samuel Peacock (Donald Meek), Lucy Mallory (Louise Platt), Dallas (Claire Trevor) and the Ringo Kid (John Wayne).

wounded, a captive Indian – all the data a spectator familiar with the Western genre requires to understand the story framework.

Again, the technique is one that Ford used on occasions throughout his working life. While *The Man Who Shot Liberty Valance* does not have such a long non-dialogue opening, it is based on a combination of three basic shots without speech to set up the narrative. An 'Iron Horse' period train is seen crossing a typical Western landscape, indicating a journey. A man is shown, and the spectator can surmise that he is waiting for the train to arrive. The iconography confirms the Western setting. The audience is shown the station, with the signpost 'SHINBONE' prominent, the train arrives and the frame confirms that the man is waiting for it. A man and a woman alight. So far the only sound has been the diegetic noise of the train itself. The narration is tightly controlled, working entirely by suggestion. The audience is presented with bits of detail that need to be assembled, putting those spectators well versed in the genre at their ease. There is, then, however, a slightly disconcerting development. Despite the apparent conventionality of the iconography within the Western tradition, when the three characters are seen together it is striking that they are all older than might be expected. This is a return journey, time will be a factor both in the narrative and the narration. The dialogue, when it does commence, affirms these ideas, but the basis has been laid visually.

Ford had mastered such methods of storytelling in the silent era, and used them with great economy and effectiveness in, for example, *Young Mr Lincoln*. When Lincoln initially becomes interested in the study of law, he is depicted in a riverside scene with his potential sweetheart, Ann Rutledge, in which they walk from screen right to screen left along the river bank. After her departure Lincoln throws a stone into the river and the camera frames the ripples, which are dissolved into ice on the water. Lincoln next appears in the spot where the earlier scene began, but it is now snow-covered and contains Ann's gravestone. In a few silent seconds a passage of time and an untimely death have been narrated. Lincoln speaks to Ann's grave and 'allows' her to decide whether or not he should pursue his law studies, by seeing which way a stick falls. It points right to left, the direction he and Ann had followed. Cut to the town of Springfield, where he will make his reputation, and Lincoln entering from left to right: the direction of his life has literally been changed. Movement within the frame contributes to the cohesion of the narration, editing becomes a function of the storytelling from an audience's point of view.

The Long Voyage Home is another film in which, while there is no dialogue for more than four minutes, information is still being presented throughout. This begins with a title board exposition of a philosophy of the sea, then a montage of scenes accompanied by diegetic sound, such as the fragments

Young Mr Lincoln (1939). Ann Rutledge (Pauline Moore) and Abraham Lincoln (Henry Fonda).

of radio reports indicating a wartime setting and the imminence of danger. The first dialogue an audience is aware of is too indistinct to be comprehended, until eventually Donkeyman is asked 'Anyone left the ship?' That becomes a central narrative concern.

With economic narrative circularity, and a complete disregard for verisimilitude, the press-ganged Driscoll's fate is conveyed by the newspaper headline seen through the water: 'AMINDRA TORPEDOED'. That appropriately leads into the final title board, taking the film full circle while also emphasizing the changes it has charted: 'So men like Ole come and go, and the Driscolls live and die, and the Yanks and Smittys leave their memories – but for the others the Long Journey never ends.'

The title board can be interpreted as a feature left over from the silent cinema's style of storytelling. Certainly, it is a way of conveying information quickly and concisely, but it is also an aspect of older, traditional narratives – a convention, such as 'Once upon a time', that creates a framework for telling a story. It is a formal element in narration that signifies a narrative is about to follow. In the pseudo-historical *Young Mr Lincoln* the credits are followed by a superimposed poem about Lincoln, and the information concerning place and time: 'NEW SALEM, ILL. 1832'. Ford's final full feature film, *7 Women*, includes an interesting variant on the method and illustrates that he clearly did not regard it, even at the end of his career, as an inappropriate technique. The film opens with a red superimposition over a wild landscape, carrying the data of both time and place: '1935 North China near the border of Mongolia . . . A land of feudal war lords and marauding bandit armies.' As the picture's action starts, the camera fixes on the sign: 'UNIFIED CHRISTIAN MISSION'S EDUCATIONAL SOCIETY'. A car arrives at a double gate, which is opened for it to enter, and the camera moves into the mission's compound. Without dialogue the spectator has been given all the information necessary to start the story.

A not dissimilar technique of narration is the voice-over. Again, this is a method Ford used throughout his career. *How Green Was My Valley* employs a first-person narrator, while such very different movies as *She Wore a Yellow Ribbon*, *The Wings of Eagles* and *Cheyenne Autumn* use the voice-over technique too. Ford simply used the form of narration that was most appropriate to the narrative content of any particular film. Part of his strength as a storyteller was the ability to distinguish between appropriate and inappropriate methods.

A recurring structure of classical Hollywood narration is the fourfold form: normality, rupture (an event that disrupts the normality), enigma (what/who caused the disruption and why), resolution (usually involving the re-establishment of normality, although sometimes incorporating change). A spectator might be able to anticipate the overall narrative structure, but the detail can still give pleasure, creating excitement, uncertainty and tension about the different possible routes of development. Also the pacing of a story is crucial.

A good illustration of all this can be seen in *The Searchers*. The film begins by establishing the normality of the family. Ethan's homecoming is the reason for the initial celebration, but it is presented by introducing the family members individually. The picture actually starts inside the house, as the door is opened by a woman in rear-view silhouette to reveal a typical Western landscape. A distant figure is faintly discernible coming towards the camera, and it is not until then that the first character-establishing shot – a view of the woman looking towards the distant figure – is made. A cut back to the nearing horseman is followed by the appearance of a man, probably her husband, who joins the woman on the veranda, and is seen from the same front-shot position. Cut to a side shot that runs along, rather than into, the veranda revealing two more characters, who may be daughters, and a dog. Those five figures remain in frame as a boy, presumably a son, wanders into shot. Eventually, as the distant figure nears the house, the first words of the film are spoken, as one of the daughters tells her brother, 'That's your Uncle Ethan.' The dialogue then clarifies the situation and eventually the last character in the circle, Martin, enters, apologizing for being late;

Ethan's reaction that the newcomer could 'pass for a half-breed' introduces a note of tension.

The family atmosphere is, then, not entirely harmonious, but the main narrative rupture occurs with news of the Indian raid. The bulk of the movie concerns the central related enigmas of whether or not the searchers will find Debbie, and what her fate will be if she is found. The narrative's resolution is a return to something like the initial family home and group, although with important differences. Indeed, there is an aspect of reversal, since the opening of Ethan's homecoming is parodied in the final image of his irrevocable departure. The final closing of the door ironically echoes its original opening.

A pursuit of this length in time cannot continue at one pace or in a single tone without becoming boring, and there are numerous ways, such as the flashbacks and the changing relationship between Ethan and Martin, that Ford, as storyteller, maintains narrative interest. A notably critical point is the moment when the searchers discover Debbie. 'Uncle' Ethan's intention is to kill the niece who has has lived as a squaw and is therefore in his eyes irrevocably degraded. As a quasi-brother 'half-breed', Martin's hope is to return Debbie to the family. Debbie runs away from Ethan towards a cave, and the final pursuit is filmed in a typically Fordian manner from within the cave, its mouth framing the action and the set-up from a darkened interior to the light exterior prefiguring the picture's conclusion.

The man inevitably catches the girl, and the central tension stems from whether or not he will carry out his intention to kill her. Jeremy G. Butler has commented on this climactic incident:

Ethan Edwards cradles . . . Debbie Edwards after having lifted her up above his shoulders. The lifting signifies his strength and the potential threat to Debbie, the niece he has disowned. The cradling signifies his acceptance/ forgiveness of her and refers back to an earlier embrace, when Debbie was just a girl. These signifiers – lifting, cradling – within the performance text are read and comprehended by the spectator, who is sutured into the narrative through the operation of the cinematic apparatus.

(Butler, 1991, p. 11)

This is certainly a valid observation of the visual aspects of the episode, although it might be added that Debbie's clenched fist in response to Ethan's first movement emphasizes that she thinks of him as a threat, and that as he cradles her, Debbie's hand opens up. However, the spectator is bound, 'sutured', into the narrative by other 'cinematic apparatus' too. The dialogue makes explicit the signification of the cradling when Ethan says with some tenderness, given the rough-hewn nature of the character: 'Let's go home,

Debbie.' This movement is also accompanied by a dramatic change in the non-diegetic background music. The harsh chords of the pursuit music suddenly merge into more lyrical strings. All these factors of filmic narration help to key audience response to the narrative, ensuring the spectator understands it emotionally and mentally, balancing the needs of security – knowing how to respond – with those of uncertainty and suspense: what will happen to Debbie?

The search and pursuit ends in a narrative circularity, reaffirming the values of family with which the film began, but also emphasizing that the normality regained is not exactly that which was lost. A long shot from the veranda establishes the return of the horsemen, specifically Ethan with Debbie sitting in front of him. Cut to a shot across the veranda, but now filmed in the opposite direction from the opening sequence, and of course the older Jorgensens have aged. The children have been replaced by old Mose Harper, enjoying the rewards of the comfortable rocking-chair existence he had long coveted (thematically, it is an extension of childhood security into old age, emphasized by the fact that throughout the picture Mose has been something of an 'old child' figure). Ethan carries Debbie from the horse towards the house in the manner of a bridegroom introducing his bride to her new home, although he does not take her across the threshold. For a moment the quartet of Ethan, Debbie and the Jorgensens are tightly framed together before the final movement of the movie when the family go into the home and Ethan walks back towards the wilderness.

Richard Maltby has described this kind of narrative circularity as

characteristic of Hollywood's ambivalence toward closure: put the camera on the other side of the mesa toward which Henry Fonda rides at the end of My Darling Clementine *(1946) and you have the opening shot of another Western . . . It is a means by which the cinema can both complete the individual narrative and at the same time renew the audience's enthusiasm for the repeat experience of narration as process. Narrative closure releases the viewer from the movie in full awareness that the story never really ends, and thus arouses, satisfies, and, crucially, reawakens the desire to be entertained.*
(Maltby, 1999, p. 355)

Another, perhaps more emphatic, illustration is *Two Rode Together*. The opening shot of the main character, Guthrie McCabe, who is subsequently identified as the town marshal, shows him on the veranda of a saloon balancing back in a chair, feet up on the rail. When, almost at the end of the picture, McCabe is returning home, his former deputy, the apparently rather simple-minded Ward Corbey, is seen in exactly the same position, albeit from a different angle. The subsequent dialogue reveals that Ward has taken over McCabe's status as marshal, and acquired Belle Aragon, Guthrie's erstwhile sweetheart, as his fiancée, and is now buying his smart clothes from the same trader as McCabe. While normality returned to the town after McCabe's departure on the quest to rescue white captives from the Comanches, it now excludes him. McCabe has to seek another normality, which he does by riding out of town with Elena, his new sweetheart. Ford has again accomplished the paradoxical task of synthesizing the requirements of narrative closure and continuity.

The concept of satisfying audience expectations within a framework of storytelling has a double value in courtroom dramas. The spectator expects the narrative to conclude definitively – the case is won or lost – and in films of the classical Hollywood period, justice is usually done. The enigma of the story is resolved and the spectator's sense of moral rightness is satisfied. During the process there is plenty of scope for the ups and downs of narrative: moments when the case is going well, times when it appears to be lost beyond redemption. In the former case the spectator's pleasure stems partly from the reassurance that justice will be done; in the latter instances fear prevails within the audience, as well as the morally validated characters.

The Sobchacks have written of 'narrative structures' being 'certain standard configurations like telling the story from a certain perspective' (Sobchack and Sobchack, 1987, p. 204). The courtroom drama almost invariably adopts the perspective of one character or group. That is the morally validated position, the characters the spectator knows, or believes, to be in the right. This might be an attorney prosecuting a cunning criminal attempting to escape justice, or someone accused of a crime they did not commit. Although an audience will probably be encouraged to take up a particular perspective, there can still be room for ambiguity – are they really guilty or innocent?

In comedies such as *Judge Priest* and its sequel *The Sun Shines Bright* Ford plays with the conventions of the courtroom narrative. Audiences know that the atmosphere should be sombre: after all someone's fate is in the balance and even a criminal deserves serious justice. In both films Priest is a humanitarian, Southern patrician of circa 1900 who behaves like a father and a brother, as well as an employer, to his black servant Jeff Poindexter – played in both movies by Stepin Fetchit. In the later picture, for example, the spurious prosecution of the black boy Ulysses Grant Woodford breaks down when Judge Priest allows – rather, encourages – him to show his skills as a banjoist in court. Jeff Poindexter, carried away by the mood of the courtroom, joins in on his mouth-organ, and the whole scene ends with an anarchic procession to a spirited rendition of Dixie. A satisfactory conclusion is reached, but in an entirely unconventional narrative manner.

It is significant that Ford's two strongest presentations of courtroom conflict both featured innocent defendants. He was naturally drawn to the underdog's position, the man falsely accused and generally believed to be guilty. In *Young Mr Lincoln* the eponymous hero first saves the Clay brothers, Matt and Adam, from a lynch mob who think they are murderers, and then, despite the belief of the townspeople in their guilt, saves them from execution by revealing the real murderer who happens to be giving evidence in the courtroom as a false witness. J. Palmer Cass' testimony is proved to be a lie, and then by sheer strength of accusation Lincoln breaks down the arrogant bully's self-defence until he confesses. Although justice is clearly a major theme in the movie, the court case is less important for its intrinsic value than as a demonstration of young Abraham Lincoln's own love of justice, and his determination to see it triumphant. Lincoln's reason for taking up law in the first place, according to the movie, was a moral one. Reading a law book young Lincoln comments: 'By gee, that's all there is to it – right and wrong.' This attitude is confirmed later in the movie, during the murder trial, when Lincoln and John Felder, the prosecuting attorney, indulge in a sharp exchange. Felder complains: 'Perhaps if my learned friend knew more of the law . . .', but he is interrupted by Lincoln's retort: 'I may not know so much of law, Mr Felder, but I know what's right and what's wrong.' It is an allegory of the achievement of the older Lincoln who, for Ford, freed the slaves and created the democratic USA.

Over twenty years later Ford returned to the idea of the falsely accused defendant with a more thorough treatment in *Sergeant Rutledge*. While it is intriguing that young Lincoln's sweetheart was named Ann Rutledge, Sergeant Rutledge is a Negro soldier, and no relation to Ann. A similar narrative pattern emerges, though by means of a different style of narration, as Rutledge's innocence is established through the revelation that one of the witnesses is actually the murderer. In a revelatory style of narration similar to the one adopted in the earlier film, the defending counsel, Lt. Tom Cantrell, proves that Chandler Hubble is a false witness and in a display of righteous verbal aggression forces the real murderer to break down and confess his crime. It is strong courtroom drama, the moment of triumph coming just as the false case against the defendant seemed to have been won.

There are, however, two fundamental differences between the films. First, although the movie begins and ends with Cantrell, it is not concerned with him as a character, in the manner *Young Mr Lincoln* allegorizes the president's personality and career. Justice is obviously a theme, but Rutledge – as the title suggests – is the central character, and it is his honour and integrity that provides the film's momentum. This is achieved by the second, and in this case narrational, difference – the extended use of flashback sequences. These both amplify and dramatize the courtroom debate, and by juxtaposing the present (the court martial) and the past (the events being debated) create a more complex narrative than in the earlier picture. The spectator is presented with 'facts' and different interpretations of them. The balance between Barthian fear and security, pleasure and bliss (Sontag, 1983) is maintained perfectly.

It was his all-embracing sense, and command, of the techniques of narration that made Ford such a master storyteller among film-makers. He used strong story lines, often with only a single narrative thread, but when there was a sub-plot it was always directly relevant in some way to the main narration. Also, Ford utilized all the cinematic aspects available to him: the pictures tell the story in the main, with careful framing and controlled editing; and these were supported by appropriate dialogue and the imaginative use of other diegetic sound, and non-diegetic music. All these factors contribute to Ford's success in enthralling audiences with well-told tales.

5 Conservative or subversive

In the television documentary anthology *A Personal Journey with Martin Scorsese through American Movies*, Scorsese categorizes key directors into storytellers, illusionists, smugglers and iconoclasts. Included in the first category are such film-makers as Ford, 'who work *with* the system and make it work for them' (*Sight and Sound*, June 1995, p. 22). This suggests that Ford is both a conservative, working within the system, and a potential subversive, making the system work *for* him. Although this is true up to a point, it ignores Ford's attempts to work *outside* the studio system, through the production company he and Merian C. Cooper set up, Argosy. Another aspect of the question concerns Ford's ideological position, over which there is some disagreement. He naturally sided with the underdog, but does that mean he automatically confronted the establishment powers? It might be argued that Ford was not so much ideologically committed to those he saw as oppressed and underprivileged, as romantically attracted to them, viewing social outsiders in a romantic light as high-integrity rebels – and identifying his own situation, somewhat unjustifiably, with theirs.

Certainly, in the classical Hollywood period the studio system could be very oppressive, although it is also true that Ford was given a good deal of freedom on occasions. He was allowed, for instance, to finish *The Iron Horse*, despite stretching a four-week schedule into ten weeks. This was an unusual situation for Ford, who was famed for bringing in films on schedule and within budget. Although partly caused by adverse weather conditions on location beyond Ford's control, even so it was an expensive picture and another director might well have seen the studio cut its losses after the initial four weeks. Later, it was Zanuck who encouraged Ford to be more radical in filming *The Grapes of Wrath*. Illustrations of the helpfulness of executives may be comparatively rare, but they do exist.

Nevertheless, in general, studio interference was at best unhelpful, and at worst destructive. William Darby, for example, has noted some curious editing slips in *My Darling Clementine*:

Chihuahua appears in black stockings inside the saloon when she spies on Wyatt's cards and is then bare-legged when he throws her into the horse trough moments later; Jack Pennick mysteriously replaces the first coach driver on Doc's mad dash out of Tombstone; and Wyatt goes from being unlathered to completely lathered within a moment in the barbershop when Mr Bon Ton is interrupted by the rampaging Indian Charlie.

(Darby, 1996, p. 285)

Ford was renowned for his ability to carry continuity shots in his memory, so these slips are rather more prominent than they might be under a less meticulous director.

The explanation perhaps lies with the dispute that blew up between Ford and the head of 20th Century-Fox, the redoubtable Zanuck, who was partly responsible for editing the movie. Zanuck had edited several Ford pictures extremely successfully, including *The Grapes of Wrath* and *How Green Was My Valley*. Gallagher records Ford's daughter Barbara, herself a former editor at the Fox studios, telling him in 1979: 'My father was the second greatest editor who ever lived. Zanuck was the greatest' (Gallagher, 1986, p. 464). Zanuck, though, did not like the initial shoot of *My Darling Clementine*, writing to Ford: 'You have in the film a great number of outstanding individual episodes and sequences . . . touches that rival your best work, but to me the picture as a whole in its present state is a disappointment. It does not come up to our expectations' (Eyman, 1999, p. 314). In any event, Ford's normal working method was to leave an editor as little room for manoeuvre as possible, and Zanuck was forced to reshoot some sequences (for example, in the released version a final kiss replaces Ford's original handshake leave-taking), which might explain the faulty continuity. Such actions might well annoy any director, but Ford was never gracious in receiving criticism, and the film effectively ended the close collaboration between the two men. In the previous year Ford had been in furious conflict with MGM over the studio's proposed editing of the war movie, *They Were Expendable*, made while the conflict was still raging. Five years after its release Ford was still so bitter that he claimed he had never seen the final version (although Lindsay Anderson eventually persuaded him to do so).

After these battles of 1945 and 1946 it is little wonder that Ford's own production company, Argosy, got into full gear in 1947 with *The Fugitive*. In the following five years it created a number of interesting, if not actually fine, movies, among them: *Fort Apache, 3 Godfathers, She Wore a Yellow Ribbon, Wagon Master, Rio Grande* and *The Quiet Man*. Ford's attempt at independence, however, enjoyed only relatively short-term success. The completion of a movie is merely the beginning of the process that ends with an audience watching it. Distribution and exhibition processes are also necessary, and those involve other institutions in the industry.

Argosy's first regular partner was RKO Radio, with a deal involving MGM for *3 Godfathers*. In 1950 Republic became Argosy's distributor, but as a studio it produced a lot of minor films each making a small profit and was unused to the Ford–Cooper manner of film-making. The director's natural irascibility could hardly have helped the working relationship, but Argosy had genuine grievances against Republic concerning the finances. The company's treasurer, Lee Van Hoozer, wrote to Republic about their first collaboration, *Rio Grande*: 'Both Mr Ford and Mr Cooper are deeply concerned with the financial reports for this picture' (Eyman, 1999, p. 414). Van Hoozer claimed that Argosy's share of the profits should be treble the amount handed over by Republic. The dispute dragged on, reaching its most bitter point over *The Quiet Man*. Dan Ford, the director's grandson, has observed: 'The contract called for Argosy and Republic to split the gross profits 50–50. *The Quiet Man* was, of course, an enormously successful picture. But while the money should have been raining in, it was only dribbling in. Something obviously was wrong . . . Somewhere between the theaters and Republic's accounts the money was disappearing, and John had a pretty good idea where it was going' (Ford, 1998, p. 250). The dispute rumbled on for several years, until Argosy was finally paid a considerable sum in settlement. It is no wonder that Ford was forced back into the studio system, although by then the oligarchy had begun to crumble.

He was again in the position of having to try to make the system work *for* him. The fact that Ford, at the age of seventy and beyond his commercial peak value, was able even to make a film as expensive as *Cheyenne Autumn*, at Warner Bros' cost, is a tribute to his persistence and ability to understand the system. In the event, though, he had many battles with Warners – over conception, scenario, casting, music and editing – and lost a number of them. Ford subverted the studio system to a degree, inveigling, bullying or fooling it into playing his tune – but it was not a one-sided victory, and the director often had to pay a high price for his triumphs.

Ford was to some extent a natural rebel, a subversive by temperament. Yet ideologically he had very conservative tendencies too. These are not, perhaps, incomprehensible inconsistencies within an inherently paradoxical character. He liked to associate himself with the anti-British Irish rebels, apparently sent funds to the IRA and claimed to have fugitive relatives, yet his most substantial film dealing at all with Irish politics, *The Informer*, is set in 1922 – after the creation of the Republic of Ireland in 1921 – and mainly depicts IRA infighting. Sarris finds the thematic paradox at the heart of the film difficult to accept: 'What makes *The Informer* particularly uncomfortable is Gypo's pathetic yearning to rejoin the ultra-Fordian community

– the IRA – which has been mobilised to destroy him' (Sarris, 1998, p. 180). Towards the end of his life, when young men were burning their draft cards in the USA, and anti-Vietnam War demonstrations were at their fiercest, and bloodiest, *Vietnam! Vietnam!* rejected the cause of the rebels with its commentary: 'To those in command of North Vietnam and the Vietcong the pursuit was a united Vietnam under Hanoi with a communist government. To those in South Vietnam the pursuit was to be left alone.' It is, maybe, easier to support rebels and rebellion when they are not present in the here and now.

Ford's last public pronouncement, on the occasion of his receiving the Presidential Medal of Freedom from President Richard Nixon on 31 March 1973, is recorded as 'God bless Richard Nixon'. Fewer than eighteen months later Nixon resigned over his criminal involvement in the Watergate scandal, a fact predicted by Ford's son Pat, who advised his father, in March 1973, not to be associated with Nixon. Ford was very ill and only five months from death, but it was not feeble-mindedness as such that drove him towards acceptance of right-wing authoritarian figures. Eyman observes that twenty years earlier Ford had had fraternal dealings with Nixon:

> There is a 'Dear John' letter from Richard Nixon from March 1953, thanking Ford 'for all that you did to make possible our overwhelming victory,' and inviting him to drop by anytime he was in Washington. Add to that a letter from the conservative Republican Ohio senator Robert Taft, thanking Ford for his commiseration over the party's nomination of Eisenhower. All this indicates that Ford's enthusiasm for Roosevelt and Harry Truman did not extend to Adlai Stevenson.
>
> (Eyman, 1999, p. 386)

His friendships with John Wayne and Ward Bond – in both cases going far deeper than the usual director/actor relationship – illustrate how comfortable Ford was in the company of men with right-wing tendencies. The biographers Roberts and Olson have written of Wayne: 'Disliking messages in the movies of liberal and radical filmmakers, by the early 1950s Duke was increasingly trying to make political statements in his own films' (Roberts and Olson, 1995, p. 349). Bond became president of the Motion Picture Alliance for the Preservation of American Ideals, an organization that cooperated enthusiastically with Senator Joseph McCarthy's witch-hunting HUAC. Despite his regard for Lincoln and Lincolnian concepts of liberty, freedom and equality, Ford did possess an innate conservatism that also made him authoritarian, creating some natural affinity with right-wing attitudes.

Paradoxically, though, it was the desire for personal autonomy that drove Ford to fight the studio bosses. It was, to some extent, a conflict of wills. But

Ford was a more complex character, and did have a genuine liberal streak in his personality. He became vice-chairman of the Motion Picture Democratic Committee in 1937, and, as mentioned earlier, later actively opposed McCarthyism, being instrumental in defending the liberal writer/director Joseph Mankiewicz against De Mille at the crucial Screen Directors Guild debate over the precise implementation of the anti-communist loyalty oath in 1950. In his obituary of the director, Krebs quoted Ford as having claimed: 'I'm thoroughly apolitical and nonideological. I don't think I've ever even voted in a Presidential election' (*New York Times*, 1 September 1973). This statement could well have been one of Ford's renowned obscurations. In any event many political theorists argue there is no such position as apolitical or non-ideological, that such terms are merely alternative expressions for supporting the *status quo*. In this case the essential conservatism of the position would be unconscious rather than conscious. The complexity, apparently oscillating between conservatism and subversion, is manifest in the films.

Harry Carey Jr, who acted in a number of Ford's pictures, and had family connections with the director, wrote that '[Ford's] politics fluctuated, depending on who he would like to see as president of his country, and, God, how he loved his country. The "liberals" in this town always called him a "right-winger" or a "reactionary", but he was simply a true patriot' (Carey, 1994, p. 8). Carey's view to some extent reconciles the oppositions, and certainly confirms the importance of Americanism in the canon of Ford's movies.

A recurring Fordian theme with obvious ideological overtones occurs in his first big feature, the epic that created his initial reputation in 1924, *The Iron Horse*. The central theme is the making of the embryonic modern USA in the nineteenth century. Thematically the movie can be seen as a conservative celebration of the 'American Ideals'. In terms of film-making it was certainly radical and might be interpreted as subversive of aspects of conventional cinema. Ford's dichotomous desire to be part of a tradition, the American Dream perhaps in this case, and the need to be individualist, to make new statements, or statements in innovative ways, is revealed in *The Iron Horse*, which repays some close analysis.

The Iron Horse is, of course, the railway, and the film is concerned with the construction of the transcontinental railroad, the linking of the east and west coasts and all points between by a comparatively fast and efficient means of transportation. The link was completed in 1869, just four years after the momentous Civil War had ended, marking the beginning of the concept of the full United States of America. The railway network made it possible for people to move about more easily, and opened up the western regions to migration from the east. Since European immigrants arrived by

The Iron Horse (1924). Davy Brandon (George O'Brien) centre frame.

sea at the eastern ports, the transcontinental railway made their journey westward much easier than it had been for previous generations. This was obviously important for the development of the USA, but the railroad also made it very much cheaper to transport freight, and that encouraged economic expansion. Maldwyn A. Jones, writing from the perspective of an economic historian, has observed of the USA: 'The distinctive characteristics of the new industrialization were most fully typified by the railroads. They were the key to post-Civil War economic growth and constituted the most important single economic interest in the country' (Jones, 1991, p. 300). Economic expansion was allied to population growth, and both of those to military strength.

At the beginning of the nineteenth century the USA had a population of approximately 7 million people; by the end of the century it was about 76 million, more than a tenfold expansion; and by the time Ford made *The Iron Horse*, it had exceeded the 100 million mark and was still increasing. In industrial production the output of, for example, crucial products such as crude petroleum increased between 1860 and 1920 from half a million barrels to over 440 million, while iron ore production rose from under 3 million tons to almost 70 million, out-producing every other nation in the world. It is hardly an exaggeration to say that the USA was two different countries in the nineteenth and twentieth centuries, with John Ford being born in the middle of the transition. In 1898, when Ford was three or four years old, the USA fought a successful war against Spain, and was proud to have exerted its strength against one of the old European colonial powers, becoming new global colonialists in the process. Senator Albert Beveridge expressed the celebratory expansionist mood at the time: 'Fate has written our policy,' seeing a vision in which there will be 'Great colonies, governing themselves, flying our flag', which would lead to a world covered by 'American law, American order, American civilisation' (Pearce, 1981, p. 9). Since 'Fate' had dictated events, there was nothing the rest of the world could do about it. The use of such intertitles in *The Iron Horse* as the 'strong urge of progress', 'great nation pushing Westward' and 'inevitable path to the West' clearly expresses the idea that the nineteenth-century US expansion was the fulfilment of the nation's 'Fate'.

Ford was fascinated, even obsessed, by North America's past, because that is where the present came from – history is not simply a matter of facts, it is a question of interpretation, and reinterpretation. For a first-generation American born during the critical transition period when the USA emerged from its position as one of the developing nations to vying for a global position against the old European empires, the processes of change were almost bound to be compelling. *The Iron Horse* celebrates the transformation of the nation in a truly patriotic manner.

The film is a Western and many critics have followed Jim Kitses' useful description of the genre as a 'shifting ideological . . . series of antinomies' that emanate from the basic thematic dichotomy of 'Wilderness/Civilisation' (Kitses, 1969, p. 11). The concept is applicable to many of Ford's Westerns. In *The Man Who Shot Liberty Valance*, for example, the central dichotomy is visualized in the recurring image of the cactus rose. Peter Wollen validly restates Kitses' general position: 'Ford finds transcendent values in the historic vocation of America as a nation, to bring civilisation to a savage land, the garden to the wilderness' (Wollen, 1998, p. 81). This is certainly generally valid. However, specifically in *The Iron Horse* Ford is concerned not with the transforming of the wilderness into a garden, with its associations of cultivation, but with the difference between desert and productivity. *The Iron Horse* is thematically engaged with the difference between desert – barrenness, unproductivity – and industrialization. The rails are both products of heavy industry and a means of creating industrialization. The railroad is a signifier of economic wealth and national strength and an agent of future transformation. There is, clearly, a degree of mythologizing in this kind of argument.

The general cultural assumptions – that everyone is becoming wealthier, that everything is getting better, that process means progress – tend to ignore the victims of change. The indigenous Indians are an obvious example, and while most Negroes remained desperately underprivileged, many white workers also suffered rather than benefited. The thousands of men who died actually constructing the transcontinental railroad, not only in attacks by hostile Indians but also from illness, disease and industrial accidents, were certainly among the exploited. The Indians do suffer, but in *The Iron Horse* their function is to perform as agents of conflict, rather than be shown as victims of historical processes. The past as reality, myth, legend – the re-examination of history – became a recurrent Fordian concern. *Cheyenne Autumn*, for instance, is a revisionist Western, an early entrant in that category, revising the mainstream Hollywood perception and portrayal of Indians and the historical processes. Ford's obsession with the nature of history, the present's relationship with the past, was exercised throughout his career, specifically in three flashback films: *How Green Was My Valley*, *Sergeant Rutledge* and *The Man Who Shot Liberty Valance*; and the theme arises in other films too. All are capable of being interpreted as either eulogizing or glorifying the past, or as critically examining the validity of its assumptions: of being essentially conservative celebration, or subversive questioning.

Made early in his career, *The Iron Horse*, although containing scenes both of comedy and tragedy, is essentially lyrical. The narrative thrust of *The Iron Horse* is, typically within the Ford canon, carried not by the grand overarching theme, but via the personal histories and relationships of characters. The central narrative thread tells the story of Davy, who as a boy witnesses his father's murder and is powerless to act against the main perpetrator. Much later, while with the railroad construction outfit, he meets his childhood sweetheart, who by then has become engaged to a weak, no-good character. Like many Ford narratives it is very close to melodrama – depending on dramatic coincidental meetings, the linking of different plot threads – although the setting and general iconography is Western, and it works partly by means of the astute insights into human nature. Desire for revenge and for love are not uncommon human experiences. Spectators do not always have their desires fulfilled in real life, but Davy, like many Fordian heroes, goes through the emotional processes and, though displaced from the audience's time into history, becomes a recognizable and identifiable figure in terms of basic common experience.

The Iron Horse clearly struck a chord with 1920s audiences. It was one of the most popular films of the decade in terms of box-office receipts, eventually returning more than ten times its cost, and establishing Ford as beyond doubt one of Hollywood's leading directors. William K. Everson has ascribed its commercial success to qualities that were to become common features of the director's films: 'Ford . . . loaded it with action, romance, and comedy . . . It was one of the best of the western epics and greatly influenced the railroad-building sagas made subsequently' (Everson, 1978, p. 256). *The Iron Horse* was both popular and seminal in the development of film-making – and rewards study, because it was an artistic success too.

The opening title card claimed the film to be 'Accurate and faithful in every particular of fact and atmosphere' in its re-creation of history, and a good deal of effort was put into achieving authenticity, such as the use of the original locomotives; yet it is a mythologizing celebration of nationhood that stresses some aspects of history while glossing over others. Its artistic success does not lie in authenticity, but in precisely an opposite quality – the film's skill, a typical Fordian one, at fictionalizing events.

The emphasis on the grandeur of the landscape and the epic nature of the conflict with native Indians is related to the ways cameras are used, angles fixed, editing utilized, figures placed, hundreds of extras controlled, rather than the documentary re-creation of historical reality. The rhythmic editing of the work of the rail-layers expresses the value of work undertaken in pursuit of a common purpose: these men, too, are heroes in their dedication to duty, to the job in hand. They are the civilian equivalent of the common soldiery who are celebrated for their devotion to cause in *She Wore a Yellow Ribbon* as 'the dog-faced soldiers . . . wherever they went that became the United States'. The railroad constructors and the soldiers are linked through their work of pushing back the frontier, of unifying that which had been disparate. The roughneck hero with a bristling exterior but a heart of gold is eventually developed into another of Ford's stock figures, and embodied in an individual character rather than a mass, for the crowd can be volatile and a threat as well as a reassurance – as, for instance, *Young Mr Lincoln, How Green Was My Valley* and *The Sun Shines Bright* were to show.

For Ford the visual poet, the frame had to be interesting in itself. But one of his strengths as a director was that he had little tolerance for purely pretty or lyrical shots that added nothing substantial to the film as a whole. In this sense he might be considered a radical film-maker, subverting Hollywood conventionality. Shots also needed to be appropriate to mood, action and themes. In *The Iron Horse* the rail-laying process is often photographed with the camera looking along the lines, giving a sense of perspective, of process and progress. However, when the job has been finished and the transcontinental line is at last an accomplished fact, Davy is photographed standing alone on the track, but with the rails running not from the bottom to the top of the screen, but across from left to right, with the mountains in the distance. There is a sense of completion, which is emphasized by the change of viewing angle. The spectator, like the characters, is no longer looking towards a destination, the meeting of the rails converging from west and east, for it has been achieved.

The history of the making of *The Iron Horse* provides an early illustration of studio interference. Ford was by no means alone in this, and it usually took the form of cutting, or re-editing, material – as happened later, for example, to *Cheyenne Autumn* and *My Darling Clementine*. Erich von Stroheim's epic classic *Greed* (1925) released only four months after *The Iron Horse*, was cut by over a half by the studio, to the extent that the director disowned the released version. In the case of *The Iron Horse* the interference took the opposite course, with the Fox studio insisting that additional footage be shot and incorporated. Peter Bogdanovich quotes a conversation with Ford about this aspect of the film:

> 'they had this girl whom they were paying a lot of money, and Sol Wurtzel
> [a Fox executive] said there weren't enough close-ups of her. So they got
> some other director who put her up against a wall, and she simpered. It
> had nothing to do with the picture – the lighting didn't match, not even
> the costume matched. They stuck in about twelve of these close-ups, but of
> course it ruined the picture for me.'
>
> (Bogdanovich, 1978, pp. 44–6)

In his attempts to subvert the Hollywood norm, it was a stylistic issue that Ford fought against all his career.

The roughneck common man figure who emerges from Ford's concept of the people as potential heroes in *The Iron Horse* appears in individualized prototype even before that epic film. Between 1917 and 1921 Ford made twenty-five films with the experienced actor Harry Carey. Carey was a great influence on the young director, as Ford himself acknowledged in   ·ng to Carey as his tutor in an interview with Bogdanovich, and as conf Harry Carey Jr, in conversation with Anderson. In the role of (Harry in *Straight Shooting*, for instance, Carey plays a hired gun whe the influence of the heroine Joan, reforms his life with the statem giving up killing'. In fact he then goes on to defend the farmers . contracted to kill and refuses to pursue his interest in Joan when he reaน.. that she loves another man. This is not so much conversion of personality as the development of previously suppressed, or unrecognized, traits of goodness. The Ringo Kid in *Stagecoach* is introduced as a roughneck fugitive from justice who ultimately proposes the respectability of marriage to Dallas, the golden-hearted whore. They become mirrored types, both social and moral outcasts, who can also be seen as essentially radical figures, genuine celebrations of the underdog and the socially disadvantaged. They also celebrate American individualism, characters who are not afraid to make their own decisions and take responsibility for their own actions. This can be seen either as a passive acceptance of the ideology of the American Dream or as an active rejection of American moral conformity.

A film such as *Young Mr Lincoln*, however, seems clearly to endorse the Dream. At the beginning of the movie, Lincoln has no real idea of what to do with his life; he has no burning destiny, just a general sense of decency. But it ends with the vision of a man striding out to meet his, and the nation's, destiny. Lincoln becomes an emblem of the USA itself, a youthful, idealistic nation reaching new horizons with confidence and hope – all set in a fortuitous rainstorm that Ford, flexible artist and technician that he was, shot and used appropriately. Fate was on the side of Lincoln, Ford and the USA.

Another aspect of what might be considered Ford's conservatism was his attitude to hierarchical institutions, in particular the armed services and the Roman Catholic Church. He made many films about the cavalry, and the twentieth-century army, navy and air force. Ford did make criticisms of all of them, but the general tone is one of admiration. Although *They Were Expendable* begins with the top brass rejecting the value of the PT-boats (small, relatively lightly armed, but extremely manoeuvrable craft), the movie goes on to demonstrate the visionary judgement of the lower ranks who have, and maintain, faith in them. Individuals in the armed services might indeed make mistakes, but the body of men who comprise the mass have a common goodness and knowledge that sustains the institution. But it is the institution in the first place that forges the men into a coherent body.

The dramatic irony of the initial rejection is emphasized when a retirement speech is interrupted by a radio broadcast giving news of the surprise Japanese attack on Pearl Harbor. Boots Mulcahey explains to a group of mostly very young sailors that Doc Charlie is being 'paid off' after thirty years' service: 'most of you kids got a long ways to go before you find out what thirty years in the navy means. It means service, tough and good – it means serving your country in peace and in war. Let's raise our glasses [the radio interrupts with "An important announcement"]. Oh, cut that thing off.' The moment is itself a historic one for the nation, a transition from peace to war, a defining point after which the PT-boats, and their sailors, will prove their worth in serving the country. The importance of the moment is also fixed visually, with Boots and Doc being framed statically, and from a slightly low position – one of Ford's favourite camera angles – as virtually a two-shot, although each is flanked by another character just on the edge of the screen to complete the sense of a social grouping.

It is the idea of service, of mutual dependence leading to comradeship, that gives the individual men a purpose: the man as part of the team is bigger than when he stands alone. Ford's admiration of the institutions of the armed services stems from that conviction. When Lt. Rusty Ryan is contemplating requesting a transfer from the PT-boat unit to 'a Destroyer', his commander, Lt. John Brickley, asks: 'What are you aiming at, building a [personal] reputation – or playing for the team?' Ryan stays with the team. Ford validates the team over the individual.

His attitude to the Church, priests and churches is essentially respectful, even reverential, for similar reasons. Hardly any Protestant priests or churches, or non-Christian denominations are taken seriously in Ford's movies. Even in a knock-about farce such as *Donovan's Reef*, set on a Pacific island, it is Fr Cluzeot's Catholic church that represents the joint centre of the community, along with Donovan's bar, and the islanders all dutifully and happily attend the Father's services.

In *Mogambo* (1953), Eloise Y. Kelly enters the narration as a hedonistic playgirl, eventually becoming a serious-minded suitable potential spouse for Victor Marswell, taming his selfish white-hunter immorality in the process. The critical moment occurs when the safari party stop at an African village under the influence of Fr Joseph and his wood and straw church. The camera is placed deep inside the rough church, looking out on to a large group of Africans, the arch of the open-ended building providing a typical Fordian framing. Kelly strides in from the right and the natives greet her, to which she responds with a wave. She then notices that it is a church, no matter how humble, she is passing. She stops, perhaps at first merely curious, but her posture changes and a scarf she has been fortuitously carrying is put into service as a headscarf, a traditional covering. Kelly dips her fingers into the holy water at the entrance and crosses herself. As she moves into the church, the camera cuts to a position behind her, so revealing the iconography of altar and cross. Kelly kneels in reverence and appears to be about to pray, although the shot cuts away to the other members of the group meeting Fr Joseph. Cut then to a frontal frame of Kelly on her knees, lips moving silently. Leaving the church, she joins the main group and stands reverentially before the priest, who invites her to lunch with a gesture of benediction. Some time later, with African drumming going on in the background, Fr Joseph and Kelly are shown in ritual confession. The music drowns her words, but after leaving the confessional Kelly attempts to apologize to, and befriend (unsuccessfully), her rival in love.

The episode is a very clear indication of the character's true moral worth: that the influence of the Catholic Church and its benign priest have led her to reject her hedonistic playgirl life. Just as in the armed services, the individual has become a bigger person by bonding herself with the Church and its teachings. It is difficult not to see his validation of hierarchical institutions as reflecting a conservative element in Ford's make-up. Nevertheless, this is not necessarily to argue that the word 'conservative' is being used in a derogatory sense. Many people feel that human beings are better, and happier, when functioning as part of a team.

Despite Ford's own obscurantism in refusing to discuss whether or not his vision became darker from about the mid-1950s, many critics have argued that this is the case. Jackie Place, for instance, in linking the 1956 and 1960 films has written: 'Two Rode Together is Ford's first obviously cynical Western. It is almost a remake of The Searchers in plot, structure, and thematic concerns . . . [it] represents a deliberate hollowing out of Ford's myths' (Place, 1974, p. 200). Yet it is possible to see something of this hollowing out as early as 1948. Most of Fort Apache is concerned with the vindictive and vainglorious attitudes and behaviour of Lt. Col. Owen Thursday, who overrides the advice of his second-in-command Capt. Kirby York, despite York's greater experience in Apache matters, and ignores the fact that the renegade Indians have a legitimate complaint against their government agent, in order to pursue personal prestige, promotion and a posting to Washington. In the process many ordinary and decent men are killed, and Thursday himself dies in a futile attempt at a heroic gesture. Despite all these inadequacies of character, York reports Thursday's death in conventionally chivalric terms: 'No man died more gallantly, or won more honour for his regiment.' York, and the cinema audience, know that this is a contribution to myth-making rather than a revelation of truth. To complicate the issues even further, the movie does not end with the eulogy on Thursday, but with one on the common roughneck soldiers, who 'fight over cards or rotgut whiskey, but share the last drop in their canteens'. They are the same men celebrated at the end of She Wore a Yellow Ribbon as 'the dog-faced soldiers' who created the USA.

Some interpreters have seen this as an element of cynicism on Ford's part, an illustration that myth and reality do not match. That might be a subversive position, an acknowledgement that even men accepted by history as great have been self-seeking and stupid. On the other hand, perhaps it is a conservative assessment of the past, and by implication the present, affirming the need for heroes at any price, confirming that we have to worship our leaders whatever their faults, for ordinary people need to be led. This might be taken as an essentially authoritarian view of social organization and politics.

An ambivalence remained in the films. In the final Western, Cheyenne Autumn, where sympathy clearly lies with the Indians, the German captain at Fort Robinson hides behind the credo of the Nuremberg trials – according to which, Nazi war criminals claimed they were merely following orders – by refusing responsibility for the Indians on the grounds that 'Orders are orders'. The theme can again be taken as a conflict between irresponsible leadership and the need of the individual to uphold the dictates of conscience. The conservative will obey any order; the subversive will question and if necessary challenge and even disobey.

Ford seemed never quite sure where he stood on that particular conflict of interests. There is also the question of whether it is the man or the films that is most important, or indeed the extent to which they can be separated. Post-structuralist and psychoanalytical theorists, in particular, might argue that film-makers are only partly conscious of their obsessions, motivations and prejudices. The overt themes must always be measured against the covert, those of which the director is not aware. In Ford's case there is also the problem of whether the changing social and political climate affected his attitudes, consciously or otherwise, or if he just got older and cared less. Place's argument that the director slid into cynicism can be juxtaposed with Sarris' assertion: 'Ford never lost his faith in the benign drift of American history' (Sarris, 1998, p. 161). Clearly, the films require further analysis. That is part of their continuing interest.

6 Entertainer or ideologue

It is a commonplace belief, especially among left-wing political theorists, that everyone holds an ideological position, whether they are aware of it or not. We are all in some way products of the political, social and cultural framework in which we have been brought up and live. This creates attitudes and belief systems that determine activity. In some cases individuals will subscribe to that framework because it is to their own personal advantage; other people might rebel against it because they see it as unfair and unjust. Nevertheless, members of the latter group are still influenced by the basic framework, for it is that which they attempt to subvert. The majority of people in society, the theorists maintain, are likely to be passive, simply accepting the *status quo* as a natural feature of collective life. The most dangerous position, it is argued, is one in which the individual rejects the idea that she or he does hold ideological beliefs, and is unconscious of the fact that beliefs and attitudes are social and cultural constructs rather than natural, and therefore inevitable, factors in the organization of life. Clearly, films are an important aspect of cultural construction, either in supporting a *status quo* or subverting it. Ford, of course, was a member of society and therefore influenced by the prevailing belief systems. But as a film-maker he was also contributing to them. This perspective produces an interesting view of his work.

Ford claimed to be a simple film-maker, solely an entertainer, holding no ideological position. Does this mean he unconsciously subscribed to the *status quo*? Certainly, there are many Fordian pictures that can be so interpreted. The Indians in *Stagecoach*, for instance, are mere ciphers. Not one of them is individualized – unless we count the anonymous brave who leaps onto the team of galloping horses, only to be shot by Ringo. But even he has no name and sinks back into the amorphous mass who are driven off at the first sound of the approaching cavalry's bugle. It is just an entertainment picture, carrying no intended ideological message, yet it obviously asserts the superiority of the small group of white travellers over the hundreds of attacking Indians, who do not even have the intelligence to shoot the coach's horses (though that, of course, would have ruined the narrative). The movie also asserts the rightness and power of the US army, in its protection of women, children and the vulnerable in general. In these ways the film becomes ideologically charged, whether or not Ford was conscious of his attitudes and beliefs.

The situation is complicated because in the areas in which Ford did have a conscious intention, the films tend to be subversive. For example, the real villain of *Stagecoach*, it can be argued, is the apparently respectable banker, and the sheriff himself is complicit in Ringo's escape from the processes of law. There are also the social conscience films of that period – *The Grapes of Wrath* and *How Green Was My Valley*, for instance – that raise the question of whether Ford was a maker of movies without an ideological awareness, but which therefore contributed to the *status quo*, or was, despite his denials, consciously expressing radical ideologies.

With regard to those cultural outsiders, Indians, Ford claimed to have a friendly working relationship. Monument Valley, which belonged to the Navajo, was his favourite location, and Ford is said to have paid the Indians relatively generously whenever they appeared in his films. In the main, however, they were cannon-fodder, from *The Iron Horse*, through *Stagecoach* to *She Wore a Yellow Ribbon* and the 1950s up to *Sergeant Rutledge*. Nearly forty years of portraying Indians as desperate savages shot down in their hordes. From such evidence it can certainly be argued that Ford, deliberately or otherwise, affirmed the right of the white settlers to rule the North American continent, justifying the use of force when necessary. All this, of course, was simply part of the Western genre. Audiences expected no less, and it might be said that in entertainment pictures would not have accepted any other approach at the time. To that extent, Ford was tied into the culture in which he was working.

By the early 1960s the cultural climate was changing. *Cheyenne Autumn* can be seen as both a response to that change of consciousness and a contribution to the continuing transformation. In the film the Indians are both the victims and the heroes, embarking on an epic journey from a southwestern reservation back to their ancestral homeland in the north, succeeding only at the terrible price of near decimation. It is Ford's longest movie, lasting anywhere between two and a half and three hours depending on which version is shown, and is itself conceived on an epic scale.

On its release in London, Kenneth Tynan described the picture, as 'a large and leisurely Western', also noting that 'Its viewpoint is passionately pro-Indian' (*Observer*, 18 October 1964). That was certainly Ford's conscious ideological intention. The preproduction notes he and his son Pat wrote are clear: 'The basic premise of *Cheyenne Autumn* is to dramatize the Indian side

Cheyenne Autumn (1964). Chief Tall Tree (Victor Jory) flanked by his sons Dull Knife (Gilbert Roland) and Little Wolf (Ricardo Montalban).

of the conflict. The Cheyenne are not to be presented as heavies, nor are they to be ignorant misguided savages' (Ford, 1998, p. 297).

Some of the critics who dislike the movie have observed that Ford was nearly seventy when he made it, and that his intermittent illnesses during shooting reveal a loss of interest in the project. While it is true that on a few occasions the associate director/second unit director, Ray Kellogg, or the main star actor, Richard Widmark, took charge of direction, it remains essentially and pre-eminently a Ford film. It is a fact too that shooting overran schedule, which was unusual for a Ford picture, but that was caused partly by unseasonably bad weather at the location sites. There was also tension on set between the director's son, Pat, and the producer, Bernard Smith, which obviously soured the atmosphere. The assassination of John F. Kennedy while the crew were on location hardly lifted the clouds.

Apart from the murder of a very popular president, such difficulties, however, are not uncommon in the complex business of film-making, and Ford's own commitment to the movie went back almost ten years, to the novel's publication in 1953. Significantly, perhaps, his initial treatment of the novel by Mari Sandoz was completed with Dudley Nichols shortly after *The Searchers*. Two factors were involved in the project's resurrection: the different sociocultural climate initiated by the civil rights movement, and Ford's partnership with Bernard Smith. The two men formed the production company Ford–Smith, which to some extent paralleled Ford's partnership with Cooper in Argosy. Dan Ford described Smith as: 'a calculating businessman and a tough negotiator. Extremely well connected, he moved among Hollywood's elite like a Medici prince' (Ford, 1998, p. 296). It was Smith, the almost perfect foil for Ford, who was able, with the director, to convince Warner Bros. that the time (the early 1960s) was commercially ripe to readdress the cinema's treatment of Indians by investing $4.2 million in *Cheyenne Autumn*.

In the event the film was not a great commercial success, and subsequently even Fordian enthusiasts have expressed serious doubts about it. Gallagher has written of the film: 'Viewed almost always from immense physical distance . . . the individual Cheyenne are purely iconic, recalling *The Fugitive*'s most abstract moments. Their story . . . appears virtually in subtext' (Gallagher, 1986, p. 433). Eyman too has commented: 'The film is full of static shots that all seem to last too long. It's sincere but unfelt; Ford is too tired to summon any energy or emotion, and the way the script is structured, the audience is expected to feel the tragedy of a people they don't even know' (Eyman, 1999, p. 510). Anderson, who disliked all the late films, claimed that he had never managed to sit through all of *Cheyenne Autumn*. On the other hand, inevitably, an anonymous initial London reviewer headlined his piece: 'A John Ford Film that Recalls His Greatest Days' (*The Times*, 15 October 1964).

The film starts with 286 Cheyenne, of whom, clearly, only a few will be developed. They share the film with the sympathetic white characters of Capt. Thomas Archer (the soldier), Carl Schurz, Secretary of the Interior (the politician) and Deborah Wright (the Quaker schoolteacher). As these characters are played by Richard Widmark, Edward G. Robinson and Carroll Baker respectively – in part the box-office leads – they have significant roles if for no other than commercial reasons. James Stewart appears too, as Wyatt Earp, albeit in one of those incongruous Fordian comedy episodes, and can hardly be termed a lead – indeed, the studio at one time cut the Earp scenes from the released version.

The Indians are often photographed at a distance. This is partly due to Ford's anathema for the practice of inserting close-ups regularly, and partly because the landscape panoramas emphasize the nature and sweep of the 1,500 mile journey (various commentators, ignoring the narrative voice-over, diversely describe it as 1,200 or 1,800 miles). It is a technique Ford used successfully in his first epic, *The Iron Horse*, and saw no reason to change.

Ideas of distance and time are reinforced by the long-held shots of baking desert and snow-covered mountains. Although the photography of the land-scape in particular is stunning – William Clothier was nominated for an Oscar as cinematographer – there are no pretty pictures for their own sake. The scenery is breathtakingly beautiful, but it is also hostile. Ordinary white men who patrol this territory are heroes too – the 'dog-faced soldiers' Ford often celebrated for their feats of endurance and commitment to duty. This consciously ideological point is also made clear in the original treatment notes: 'The Army is to be portrayed as an underpaid, undermanned force all but forgotten on a distant frontier; a group of dedicated professionals trying to keep the peace despite Washington's mismanagement' (Ford, 1998, p. 297).

Ford projects the Cheyenne's case partly by showing the ignorance, greed and contempt of many of the white men, partly by depicting the dignity in suffering of the Indians and partly by displaying their human frailties. Although there is warfare between Indians and the white soldiers, it is mainly caused by a minority of powerful men who behave stupidly or irresponsibly. The doctor at Fort Robinson who attempts to save an Indian child's life and the soldier who rebels against the opportunism of the fort's commander and deposes him are essentially on the side of the Cheyenne, recognizing that injustice has been done to them. The film works by putting the Indians' point of view, but without merely and simplistically reversing the normal good/bad categories of Indians and whites. Both races reveal good and bad impulses, in general terms and within individual characters.

The vast majority of the 286 Cheyenne are bound to be 'iconic', but Ford attempts to show the Indians, at least partially, from their own point of view. The initial conception, as recorded by Pat Ford for Smith, again illustrates this:

'My father and I are agreed that the Cheyenne should not speak English in the picture. They should serve, in his words, as a "Greek Chorus." Since lack of communication was one of their chief causes of trouble it would be ridiculous to show them speaking the national language.'

(Ford, 1998, p. 297)

This was advanced thinking in the early 1960s, but it was also an entertainment film, and immediate verbal communication between Indian and white leaders was considered necessary (as opposed to the use of translators), so the former speak in a kind of cinema-Indian.

It is perhaps the ancient classical allusion to a 'Greek Chorus' in the context of a Western that has worried some critics, who maybe see it as a warning of pretentiousness. Nevertheless, *The Times* reviewer quoted earlier, while noting that 'characters are reduced, deliberately, to heroic hiero-glyphics of attitudes', also wrote of the film having 'warmth and intimacy . . . [an] air of personal identification'. The fact that the Indians are not entirely, or maybe not at all, idealized or sentimentalized is a contributory aspect. The leading Indians exhibit human frailties, which to some extent they share with a number of the white characters.

Although, for instance, Tall Tree's resolution is admirable when he stands all day in the hot sun waiting for the government delegation, which never arrives, refusing both assistance and water when he eventually falls to the ground, there is also a measure of obstinacy in the old chief's actions and attitudes. The film's narrative concentrates on the selfishness and crass stupidity of the politicians and bureaucrats who allow weather conditions and attendance at a ball to come before their civic duty to protect and care for the Indians. Nevertheless, Tall Tree's own lack of flexibility prefigures his bad judgement later when he chooses his less conciliatory son to be his successor, at a time when there was still the possibility of avoiding the kind of catastrophe that ultimately overtakes this particular group of Cheyenne.

The filming emphasizes the crucial nature of the scene. During the journey northward the ailing Tall Tree travels in a cradle, pulled along the ground by a horse, which is mostly shot from standing eye level, the downward camera angle stressing his age and infirmity. A long shot of the main party straggled out across a rocky desert landscape, beautiful but harsh, fades into a closer, lower-angled shot of Tall Tree as he is pulled along, framed behind a horse's white legs so that the shadow of the rider falls across the old man, heightening the effect of the brightness of the surrounding sunlight. As the horse moves forward, out of frame, the cradle stops, although the characters and horses in the background keep moving, which draws attention to the significance of the chief's cradle, now almost centre screen. Spanish Woman bends down toward Tall Tree, and they are given a two-shot close-up, al-though horses continue to pass between the camera and the human figures. The camera is now at ground level, encouraging audience identification with, and emotional participation in, the scene. Yet the movement behind the protagonists, and particularly between the audience and characters, is distracting, as is the fact that the chief is speaking in his own language.

The episode clearly has significance, yet it is presented in a deliberately disorientating way. It is not a conventional deathbed scene: there is too much light, movement and confusion. When the chief's sons, Little Wolf and Dull Knife, appear in response to Spanish Woman's calls of distress, the camera shifts to an even lower position. The new shot presents the chief slightly from below, and very close to the camera, with the two sons imme-diately behind him and the woman positioned at the edge of the screen, next to them. The effect is to distort the three male figures to almost gigantic proportions, giving them a mythic quality at this vital moment of the transference of power. Tall Tree momentarily rises a little, marking the significance of his actions, but as the expected heir holds out his hands to receive the symbolic package denoting chiefship, Tall Tree pushes it into the unexpectant hands of the other son. The sons' faces register disappointment and pleasure respectively. Thematically the older, but perhaps not necessarily wiser, generation had implicitly chosen confrontation rather than conciliation for the immediate future.

No matter how justified, or understandable, the Cheyenne's journey, it is also impossible. The group suffers from hunger, exhaustion and sickness, factors that inflict more casualties than the army. Eventually, in Nebraska, halfway through the journey, 'the Cheyenne nation broke apart', in the words of the voice-over narrator. By the time Fort Robinson is reached it is too late for conciliation: the faceless power-mongers in Washington have decreed that the Cheyenne must be placed under restraint and treated like criminals. In the face of such white rigidity, despite the pleas for flexibility from Archer and Deborah, the peaceable Indians rebel violently.

The Cheyenne also suffer from those recurrent white problems of vanity, sexual lust and jealousy. Red Shirt, son of little Wolf is a case in point: it is his impetuous and vainglorious shooting that foils the attempted ambush, and his coveting of one of the new chief's wives that leads to his own death in a duel.

The Indians are not perfect, they make mistakes and have emotional and intellectual weaknesses. However, they also display an intelligence their precursors in *Stagecoach* lacked. When they return voluntarily to the custody of the army in Fort Robinson, it is in the hope that Deborah will be able to intercede on their behalf with the authorities, but they have the wit to smuggle in weapons too, just in case. The Cheyenne save themselves from a cavalry attack by stampeding the army's horses, a neat illustration of Ford's self-reflexivity, since in *She Wore a Yellow Ribbon* Capt. Nathan Brittles had cleverly forestalled an Indian attack on the cavalry by stampeding the enemy's horses. When the Cheyenne display the same sharpness of mind as a character played by a white icon like John Wayne, it is obvious that some thematic and ideological significance is involved, as Darby has observed: 'In a kind of dialectic movement, the Cheyennes are given qualities that belonged to the cavalry in Ford's earlier films' (Darby, 1996, p. 258). It is possible to draw such a conclusion partly by the intertextuality of the stampede incident, but also by the way the Indian fleeing from the murdering cowboys leaps across an abyss on his horse to secure his escape, just as Sergeant Tyree had effected an escape from pursuing Indians in *She Wore a Yellow Ribbon*.

Whatever the Indians' defects or strengths in *Cheyenne Autumn*, it is several of the white characters who are actually malevolent. While the Cheyenne have a concept of community, perhaps Red Shirt apart, some of the whites are entirely self-seeking. These range from the Washington characters to those of the West. The politicians' delegation gives priority to a ball over the Indians's plight, while the capitalists who invade Carl Schurz's office include 'western railroad tycoons, mine-owners and land speculators – all such people to whom Indian scares meant lost dollars'. Newspapers extravagantly exaggerate the numbers of Indians involved ('no one asked how many Indians had escaped, the word Cheyenne was enough') and their alleged ferocity: the actual figure of 'nine soldiers killed' escalates into 'twenty-nine, fifty-nine, sixty-nine . . . a hundred and nine'. One reason for this is ideological: fear of the 'Red Man'; another is profit: greater savagery sells more newspapers. There is a wry twist on journalistic attitudes when a Denver editor informs his staff that as all the other papers are printing atrocity stories, so that 'they aren't news anymore', they will adopt a new approach: 'From now on we're going to grieve for the Red Man'. The ultimate ideology is the pursuit of sales, and therefore profit.

The commander of Fort Robinson, the Prussian Capt. Wessels, although he begins to exhibit insane Nazi-like behaviour, is also a man who has tried to understand the Indians, and owns books (in German) about indigenous cultures. He regrets having to lock up the Cheyenne, having initially welcomed them with the instruction, 'make them comfortable'. Wessels, however, has two basic personality weaknesses: ambition and insecurity. In these there are parallels with Red Shirt. Ambitious to be a great warrior and lover, he lacked the security of self-belief that would have ensured self-restraint and the patience to wait for the right time. Wessels comments when the Cheyenne first arrive: 'This will make me a major.' When he receives the unjust, and unwise, instruction from his commanders hundreds of miles away, he simply comments 'Orders are orders', and later to Spanish Woman: 'They must obey just as I obey.' Wessels lacks the self-confidence to countermand the instruction, creating a philosophical rationale for the insecurity of his temperment: 'I'm just the instrument of an order – an order I don't agree with . . . What would be this world without orders? Anarchy!'

Within the movie's dialectic, the spuriousness of this argument is challenged at least twice. Archer tells Schurz: 'At Fort Robinson I've seen respect for superior authority gone stark raving mad.' The captain retails the horrors of the situation in a sustained take, the camera positioned behind Schurz's left shoulder, thus placing Archer in a prime, and dominant, position. This adds to the authority of Archer's speech, and perhaps also gives it directorial validation. Schurz's subsequent response is to walk over to a portrait of Lincoln hanging on the office wall. As the Secretary for the Interior addresses the portrait as 'old friend', his face is reflected in the picture's glass, alongside Lincoln's, surely a Fordian endorsement of any action Schurz might subsequently take.

Immediately after the carnage that occurs as the Cheyenne break out of confinement, and surrounded by corpses, Second Lt. Scott bitterly asks Wessels, 'Has authority been sufficiently *obeyed*, sir?' Scott asks this question from an ideologically privileged position, since earlier in the picture he was overeager to pursue and arrest, or kill, Cheyenne, telling Archer: 'Thank God . . . I've waited since I was ten years old for this chance' and later explaining that his father had been murdered in an Indian massacre. Scott is a man who begins the adventure as an avenger, but after recognizing the inhumanity meted out to the Cheyenne, discovers the deeper humanity in himself. Although Scott is not one of the main central characters in the film, he is sufficiently important for the echoes of Ethan Edwards to be clear. Another wry side-reference is related to the fact that the part of Scott was taken by John Wayne's son, Patrick.

Perhaps the closest specific echo of *The Searchers* is the incident in which two starving Cheyenne beg four cowboys for food. One Indian is shot and scalped (the other is pursued, but escapes by leaping an abyss). This is an abominable crime and mutilation against a defenceless man begging for charity. The white man is committing an atrocity worse than the Indian: it is an act of pure ideological hatred. During the final assault on the Comanche village in *The Searchers*, Ethan runs down a defenceless and harmless Indian woman before riding his horse into Scar's tepee and scalping the corpse. It is an act of ideological hatred, just like the shooting out of the dead Comanche's eyes, but in this case it is complicated by carrying the weight of personal vengeance.

It is possible to see *Cheyenne Autumn* as Ford's apologia for his lifetime's apparent abuse of the Indian. A number of critics interpreted it thus, prompted by one of Ford's own reported comments on the movie: 'I've killed more Indians than Custer, Beecher and Chivington put together . . . I wanted to show their point of view for a change' (Bogdanovich, 1978, p. 104). Like many of Ford's statements this is true up to a point. A great many Indians have been killed in his movies, but with the notable exception of *Stagecoach*, there has usually been some attempt, if only by implication, to present an Indian point of view, to project them as something other than totally barbaric savages or simply cannon-fodder.

Even as early as the first epic, *The Iron Horse*, long before society in general had developed any sensitivity about the treatment of the indigenous population of North America, there was a nod in the direction of an understanding tolerance. The Indians do attack in the traditional style, and are not much differentiated as individuals, but they are led (astray) by a selfish, greedy and unscrupulous white man, the murderer of young Davy's father. It is a brutal killing committed solely in the interests of the profits to be made from land speculation.

The theme recurs in the pictures made after the Second World War, with the variation that the source of the evil is the corrupt, and corrupting, Indian agent. There is a historical reality behind this theme, as the historian Dee Brown has confirmed:

> *during the 1870s and 1880s many Indian tribes did leave their reservations because of poor treatment by the government. Historically, Indian agents were political appointees, and often they were corrupt. In addition, many knew nothing of the tribes they were sent to oversee.*
>
> *(Carnes, 1996, p. 152)*

This is more or less York's contention when, in *Fort Apache*, he notes that Cochise's discontent began shortly after the arrival of the agent Silas Meachum, the nominee of 'the Indian Ring . . . the most corrupt political group in our history'. In that movie it is the new commander, Col. Thursday, who 'knew nothing' about the Indians in his territory. In comparing the Apaches of the region to what he calls the great nations of 'the Sioux and the Cheyenne', he refers to the former as 'cowardly digger Indians'. Meachum cheats the Indians and sells them rifles, both provoking and making possible their rejection of the reservation treaty; while Thursday underestimates the enemy, a cardinal military error, and rationalizes breaking York's promise to Cochise by describing the chief as an 'illiterate barbarian . . . a savage'. These two representatives of the US government do not inspire respect or trust in either the film's characters or spectators.

Similarly, Karl Rynders, in *She Wore a Yellow Ribbon*, sells rifles to the rebellious Indians. His greed leads to his downfall, when, by haggling for a greater profit, he is murdered by his potential customers, who then loot the weapons. It is a simple moral lesson – but the more important one is that Indian unrest has a justifiable basis, even if their subsequent murdering of innocent settlers and killing soldiers who are simply doing their duty are unjustified. That justifiable basis stems from the government's dereliction of its responsibility to ensure the Indians are treated decently and fairly, and the corrupt greed of specific selfish and devious individuals.

Both Cochise in *Fort Apache* and Pony That Walks in *She Wore a Yellow Ribbon*, are honourable chiefs. Interestingly, in view of the approach to language in *Cheyenne Autumn*, Cochise speaks mainly in Spanish, which is translated by Sgt. Beaufort. This factor, the black and white photography, the stillness and slight upward tilt of the camera when he is speaking and

She Wore a Yellow Ribbon (1949). Capt. Nathan Brittles (John Wayne).

the pure reasonableness of his argument endow Cochise with a dignity none of the white characters possess. While the warrior-leader Cochise holds power over his own people, as an old chief who is losing his power, Pony That Walks' situation is more difficult. The young brave, Red Shirt, is gaining influence, and like his namesake in *Cheyenne Autumn* is spoiling for an outright war. Pony That Walks regrets the approaching war in a speech to Capt. Nathan Brittles: 'Many will die . . . Young men do not listen to me

. . . Too late, Nathan . . . We are too old for war.' In reply to Brittles' 'Old men should stop war', the old chief simply reiterates: 'Too late.'

In the event it is Brittles who saves the situation by ordering the cavalry to stampede the Indians' horses. Bereft of them the Indians have no choice but to submit to the authority of the army. Nevertheless, Brittles recognizes, and accepts, the reality of their condition and the genuineness of their grievances. As the Indians begin to walk back to the reservation, Brittles orders Lt. Pennell: 'Follow a mile behind them, walking hurts their pride. Your watching'll hurt it worse.' Pony That Walks may be a rather pathetic, impotent figure, and Red Shirt a hothead, but Indian dignity is restored somewhat by the army's recognition of their basic humanity.

Although the Indians are not so specifically motivated in *The Searchers*, it is made clear that their lifestyle is threatened. Ethan, coming across a herd of buffalo in the snow, shoots one for meat, but then continues to shoot at them with the sole purpose of driving them away, explaining with bitter satisfaction: 'They won't feed any Comanche this winter.' When Martin protests, Ethan knocks him down, and is so obsessed with the business of driving the herd away that he fails to hear the cavalry bugle that signifies the nearness of the Indian village for which he has been searching. Martin is used as a register to guide the audience's response; he is shocked by Ethan's obsessive hatred to the point of incomprehension, writing of the incident later to Laurie: 'Something happened I ain't got straight in my own mind yet.'

In *The Searchers* it is not so much that the Indians have dignity and honour, but rather that many of the white men behave with the savagery conventionally associated with the 'Red Man'. In addition to Ethan's personal racism there is an endemic white cruelty. The bugle that interrupts Ethan's stampeding of the buffalo, for instance, leads the characters to an Indian village destroyed by the cavalry. Marty again registers common human incomprehension at the carnage, and on seeing the corpse of his quasi-squaw, Look, comments: 'Why did them soldiers have to go and kill her for, Ethan? She never did anybody any harm.' It appears to be murder and destruction simply for the sake of it.

The decimation of the buffalo herds was historically a major factor in the Indian wars. The animals were plentiful, and when hunted by bow and arrow mainly for meat amply supplied the indigenous population, but the arrival of white men with rifles totally changed the natural balance. This feature of the racial and cultural conflict also occurs in *Cheyenne Autumn* when an Indian child draws a very rudimentary picture of the animal she cannot remember. The point is emphasized by Spanish Woman, who explains that they will soon run into buffalo and 'our bellies will be full again'. On reaching the buffalo prairie, however, the scene is one of desolation as the voice-over narrative fills in the details:

'And then in one tragic instant, after five hundred miles and many weeks of desperate flight, hope was gone. The white hunters had been there first, slaughtering the buffalo not for food – but for hides. The hungry Cheyenne now stood alone.'

The disappearance of the buffalo both provides a rationale for the Indians' violent struggle and also illustrates the futility of warfare in which many young men will die. Whatever the outcome of battles, the old economic and cultural infrastructure has been destroyed, a return to the good days of the past is impossible. *Cheyenne Autumn* registers regret rather than anger.

For theorists this raises an ideological enigma. Ford certainly presents Indians in a somewhat sympathetic and tolerant manner, especially given the conventions and general cinematic expectations of the period. It is, however, unclear whether this is a conscious ideological stance, an attempt to subvert dominant ideologies concerning indigenous peoples, or merely something that springs out of his desire to tell a good story – by complicating the standard narrative format Ford introduces more conflict and therefore greater drama and interest into the films. His apparently overt ideology of liberal sympathy covers, it might be argued, a deeply conservative one in which the only – or at least, main – pursuit is that of entertainment. In providing audiences with a vaguely sympathetic view of Indians, the argument might run, Ford actually confirms, by failing to directly challenge, potentially racist attitudes in the predominantly white spectators. If indeed such a theoretical approach is valid, it is because the films do not concentrate on the subordinate position imposed on the Indians, but on the liberal nature of such characters as Capts. York, Brittles, Archer, the redeemed Second Lt. Scott (all decent soldiers doing a difficult job as well as they are able) and Secretary of the Interior, Carl Schurz, that rare thing an honest politician, who asks the cavalry commander the unanswerable question: 'Do you like killing Indians – women, children?'

On the other hand, the murderer who masquerades as an Indian, Lt. Col. Thursday and Rynders are all punished by death, while Capt. Wessells goes insane. Within this moral scheme, then, the films appear to move from condemnation of the abuses to affirmation of the essential goodness of white humanity and divine justice. *The Searchers*, for instance, ends with the voluntary exile of the racist Ethan, shut out from the warmth of the reunited settler family. The punishment for his brutal attitude is to be cast out from the joys and benefits of civilization; while for her suffering, Debbie is compensated by the gift of those very features of life.

Is it overt ideology, demanding justice for the underdog; covert ideology, subscribing to a view that the existing order of things is natural; or mere entertainment? But then the theorists argue that ideological beliefs permeate all culture, and that unadulterated entertainment cannot exist. Even if Ford thought he had no ideological position, that all he was doing was conveying enjoyable narratives, the films nevertheless have a hegemonic weight: they must, by their nature, either *affirm* or *challenge* the way life is, or appears to be. Looking at the films from an ideological perspective reveals contradictions and complexities, raising important and difficult questions about his work. Was he a 'mere entertainer', or was he by the very nature of the relationship between the industry and the culture conveying ideological views? Ford himself would say something to the effect, as he did to many interviewers, that he did not understand the question. But that does not mean it should not be asked.

7 Unconscious racist

Racism is an aspect of ideology, a belief system. Someone who is unaware that they have an ideology may not be conscious that they also have prejudices: while they do not *deliberately* set out to be biased, they neverthess interpret their experiences of life in a certain prejudicial manner. For example, a person who accepts as a fact of nature the superiority of their race is likely to perceive encounters with 'inferiors' in a particular light. If the inferior is thought to behave subserviently, that is a 'natural' state of affairs. If they object to being treated as such, they are regarded as aggressive or disagreeable; behaviour which in the racist's eyes, merely confirms their prejudices.

Movies, as an important element of popular culture, might either be complicit in this process or are able to challenge it, but only if the film-maker is aware of their own views. Many directors' prejudices may find their way into their pictures unconsciously, on the grounds that they are simply presenting life as they see it. One example of this is the use of stereotypical characters.

In general, the movies have presented a stereotypical portrait of the Indians (a fact that is also true for the majority of the white/black/brown/yellow characters in most movies). Their territory also resonates with the stereotype. Stereotyping, however, contains more than a single factor. Innumerable Westerns contain the line 'We're in Indian country', which is both a dangerous and an attractive place to be. Dangerous because the indigenous population is often depicted as hostile, attractive because of its value – for railroad building, mineral and metal extraction, cattle or arable farming – or just because it is the frontier and must be opened up, the wilderness that must be civilized. Indian country can also be exotic, generating both the allure and the fear of the unknown. The imaginative concept of Indian country is, perhaps, more important than its actual reality. The stereotype sets off a response in the spectator that will be directed by the context. Indians may be hostile or friendly, their territory may be attractive or dangerous, depending on the specific circumstances. One of the features of stereotyping, however, is that to some extent it lessens the individuality, the essential humanity, of characters in films, and people in real life. It has been argued that this encourages the conviction that such characters/people need to be controlled.

In general terms Indian issues were not, however wrongly, considered vital during most of Ford's working life. Indians themselves disappeared, as it were, from immediate cultural view, existing mainly as historical cinematic phenomena. Black people, however, were very evident, even before the post-Second World War demonstrations. They were generally regarded by the white majority (not every individual white person by any means, of course) as a threat that had to be controlled. Even though nominally equal, black people were generally considered to be inferior. This feeling of superiority validated white supremacy. While the film-maker has the opportunity to educate audiences, he or she is also an entertainer and must not risk alienating the public with unpopular ideas. In any event a film that antagonizes its spectators is hardly likely to educate them. As a white anti-racist film-maker, who was also a product of white supremacist culture, Ford was clearly in an ambiguous situation regarding black characters.

He first featured black characters in *Just Pals* as early as 1920. While they only appear as extras, the surprising factor about their presence at all is that the film is set in Wyoming, by no means an area with particular black associations in popular culture – unlike the deep South. Ford enjoyed a professional association with the Negro who acted under the vaudeville name of Stepin Fetchit from the 1929 *Salute* – for which, ironically, the man who was to become John Wayne was his personal dresser – to the *The Sun Shines Bright* in 1953. So Ford was always aware of the existence of black people, although he was not entirely able to avoid stereotyping. His black characters up to 1960, and perhaps beyond, remain subordinate.

Nevertheless, Ford was not afraid of introducing emotive and controversial aspects of the treatment of black people in US society. Both *Salute* and *The Sun Shines Bright* contain racist lynch mobs, as did *Judge Priest*. The controversial nature of the subject matter is attested to by the fact that the studio cut nearly all the sequence from *Judge Priest* before it was released. One of the thematic reasons for including the incidents was as a measure of the various characters' moral worth, just as the eponymous hero in *Young Mr Lincoln* proves his own physical courage, his mental and verbal quick-wittedness and his commitment to the due processes of law by turning back a (in this case, non-racist) lynch party. In *The Sun Shines Bright* blacks and prostitutes are the town's two socially marginalized groups. Looked down on by the self-styled respectable establishment, they are also presented as essential to the community's overall welfare. As so often in Ford's movies

The Sun Shines Bright (1953). Ford on set directing Judge William Pittman Priest (Charles Winniger). Reproduced courtesy of Paramount Pictures, copyright © 2001 by Paramount Pictures. All rights reserved.

respectability is a cloak for hypocrisy, and true value lies in the outcasts (see, for example, the banker and the whore in *Stagecoach*).

While the blacks are treated sympathetically, the problem for some commentators – and spectators – is that the characters are sentimentalized in order to be presented as such. Within the conceptual framework of the political and cultural theorist Edward W. Said, such an approach 'obliterated the distinctions between the type . . . and ordinary human reality' (Said, 1995, p. 230). To represent all blacks as lazy or devious or fat or kindly or exploited is to stereotype them, whether in positive or negative terms. Once they are reduced to types, the ideological argument runs, they can be controlled, subjected to the authority of the dominant group or culture, the stereotypers. The principle is the same whether the authority is fundamentally malevolent or benevolent; it is still imposed from above. In contriving racial harmony between whites and blacks in the films Ford appears to be forcing a resolution on to the fictional conflict that is inappropriate to the real world. It might be argued that he does so by diminishing the diversity and complexity of 'ordinary human reality' into the simplistic conventions of 'type'.

Judge William Pittman Priest in *The Sun Shines Bright* treats the black characters humanely, yet we are left in no doubt as to their relative social positions. Priest defends the black youth he suspects is innocent by single-handedly seeing off the lynch mob, an act of moral and physical courage that parallels his decision to walk, at first alone, behind the funeral cortège of Lucy's prostitute mother. The judge is presented as a decent human being who by his example inspires decency in others. In speaking of the youth alleged to have committed a terrible crime, Priest tells Sheriff Andy Radcliffe: 'You take this boy to a clean cell, and take care of him.' It can be seen as a patrician's gesture, which might also be illustrated by the judge's words to the arrested youth: 'Boy, you'll have a fair trial. Race, creed, or colour – justice will be done in my courtroom!' 'Boy' and 'my' have a slightly unsettling resonance in this context, perhaps connoting possession and power, which can be abused as well as used fairly.

It could be argued that Ford had no choice given that the movie is set in Kentucky in 1905. It would have been ludicrously unrealistic to have shown blacks and whites as entirely equal. On the other hand, he did not have to set his film in that particular time and place. It might be that he had a nostalgic longing for such a society, in which inequality did not matter providing everyone behaved decently and justice was always done. If Ford held such a view, it would be at best naïve, and for some critics actually offensive, in the light of the real conditions of life for black people in the South fifty years earlier – and still in the early 1950s.

All three of the pictures so far discussed were made before the great upsurge in civil rights activity outlined in the first chapter of this book, and *Judge Priest* and *The Sun Shines Bright* were both set in the South of the turn of the nineteenth century. While *Just Pals* has no specific time setting, it resonates with late-nineteenth-century, as opposed to post-First World War, atmosphere. Ford's most complex Negro portrayal, *Sergeant Rutledge*, was made during the height of the civil rights campaign. It is a film complicated by also being a Western, and falling into the courtroom suspense genre.

Although the court-martial scenes oscillate between melodrama and typical Fordian knock-about, or tongue-in-cheek, comedy (the behaviour of the officers' wives, the relationship between Col. Otis Fosgate and the water/whiskey jug), they are interspersed with flashbacks that illustrate the bravery, integrity and dignity of Rutledge, the black cavalry sergeant accused of raping and murdering the daughter of his white commanding officer, whom he is also thought to have killed. One aspect of this dual narrative structure is to place Rutledge in juxtaposed scenes in which he is either the only black character (in the trial room), or where he appears in a mainly black community (in some of the flashbacks episodes that are full of Negroes, the sergeant's trooper colleagues). Audiences are given a strong

Sergeant Rutledge (1960). Sgt. Braxton Rutledge (Woody Strode) guarded by
Sgt. Matthew Luke Skidmore (Juano Hernandez) and an unnamed corporal.

impression of the difference between a black man in a white world, and a
black man in a black milieu. The latter is not actually an entirely black
world, since its officers are white (as is Mary Beecher), but there is a sense of
the important difference between isolation and comradeship.

The white world is not a pleasant place. Not all the whites are malevolent
racists, but most of them are self-obsessed and inane, even hypocritical.
Rutledge's calm dignity in that atmosphere serves as a strong contrast to the
prejudice or triviality of his accusers, judges and the general public. That
calmness is a manifestation of his personality and military training, which
also displays itself on the field of battle. It is related to the central Fordian
theme of duty too. Escaping from what he sees as certain hanging, Rutledge
becomes aware of an imminent Apache ambush on the cavalry patrol. His
soldier's concept of duty appears to prevent Rutledge from riding on north,
'Where I'd be free', compelling him to return and warn the patrol of the
danger.

Dramatic shots of Rutledge crossing and recrossing the river of his hopes
are juxtaposed with Capt. Shattuck's cross-examination of him. In the courtroom Rutledge refutes the suggestion that he was seeking glory: 'I wasn't
thinking brave . . . Something kept telling me I had to go back. It was like

. . . it was like – I just ain't got the words.' He is presented as a man of action, whose actions are motivated by innate qualities of virtue too deep for words. However, for the film to work, the ideas have to be articulated, and under Shattuck's hostile questioning the sergeant breaks down: 'the Ninth Cavalry was my home. My real freedom – and my self-respect . . . and the way I was deserting it, I wasn't nothing but a swamp-running nigger. And I ain't that! Do you hear me? I'm a man!' Rutledge collapses into sobbing, for the only time in the film losing his self-control, and the court is adjourned.

To some extent the scene prefigures the ultimate breakdown of the real criminal, Chandler Hubble, when he too dissolves into hysterical sobbing and confessional revelation. But of course the incidents serve quite different purposes, illustrating genuine strength of character as opposed to real weakness, and they are therefore filmed in quite contrasting styles. Rutledge is photographed close up from a slightly low position, and as the passion of his speech gets the better of him, he stands, the camera remaining where it is so that he towers on the screen. This develops the way in which he is frequently shot from a low angle throughout the picture, emphasizing his physical size and moral stature. Shot in a more conventional manner, Hubble's confession takes place against the background of the prosecutor, defender and judges. When Hubble collapses into tears he becomes physically smaller, kneeling by the witness stand and beating his fists impotently on it.

Ford's intention was to ennoble the Negro characters, particularly the star, and to create a new kind of hero. Six years later he told the French reporter Bertrand Tavernier that he had made *Sergeant Rutledge* 'about a character who was not just a nice black guy but someone nobler than anybody else in the picture' (Tavernier, 1994, p. 38). In an unusually helpful interview with Bogdanovich, the director confirmed his ideological innovation: 'It was the first time we had ever shown the Negro as hero' (Bogdanovich, 1978, p. 97). An anonymous reviewer saw the film as 'a kind of apology to the Negro race for certain things it had to put up with after the Civil War' (*The Times*, 6 July 1960). Woody Strode, the actor who portrayed Rutledge, saw the movie as something considerably stronger, and more immediate, than a nineteenth-century apologia:

> 'It had dignity . . . You never seen a Negro come off a mountain like John Wayne before. I had the greatest Glory Hallelujah ride across the Pecos River that any black man ever had on the screen . . . I carried the whole black race across that river.'
>
> (McBride and Wilmington, 1988, p. 169)

Indeed, the very casting of Strode was crucial. Warner Bros. had wanted to use either of the two big black stars of the day, Sidney Poitier or Harry

Belafonte. Both were fine actors, but might have been perceived by audiences, rightly or wrongly, as white spectator's Negroes – educated and sophisticated, absorbed into mainstream white culture. Strode, on the other hand, was not widely known as an actor – he was an athlete, somewhat roughcast but with an extremely impressive physique. Those features suited Ford's purpose. If the film was an apology, it was not so much for the immediate post-Civil War indignities imposed on Negroes as for Hollywood's treatment of them. Within Ford's own canon Strode is the complete opposite of Stepin Fetchit in both personality and physique, and given the difference of their roles that seems hardly a coincidence. Indeed, the contrast between their professional names indicates a generational shift too, from the obsequious low pun to the self-affirmative. It would have been inconceivable to sing of the latter, 'Did you ever see a mountain/Come a-walking like a man?' Rutledge, how-ever, resembles, and is frequently photographed like, a mountain.

It is an irony that the song refers to 'Captain Buffalo', since no black soldier could become an officer. 'Top Soldier' Rutledge cannot, for all his ability, progress beyond sergeant, and the film is overtly much concerned with issues of race and injustice. Rutledge runs away because he believes – with some, although not complete, justification – that no one will believe him if he tells he truth. Despite saving Mary's life, as she twice affirms at the court-martial, Rutledge tells her: 'White women only spell trouble for any of us.' A little later he observes: 'We've been hunted a long time.' The 'us' and 'we' are, of course, blacks. His observation on the great emancipator – 'It was alright for Mr Lincoln to say we were free, but that ain't so, not yet – maybe someday, but not yet' – gains greater poignancy because it has already been revealed that Rutledge was a freed slave, in 1861, before the Civil War began.

That Ford was consciously attempting to make a statement about racism is indicated by his attitude to the initial story. The scenario is credited to Willis Goldbeck and James Bellah, but the former's original concept and treatment, *Buffalo Soldier*, ended ambiguously with Rutledge's heroism in battle, but no court-martial finale. The question of Rutledge's innocence or guilt was deliberately unresolved. Two major changes that bear Ford's mark are first, the change of title from generalization to particularization: this is not just any soldier but a specific one, who also has an exemplary record and reputation. Second, the imposition of a definitive conclusion, in which black integrity, dignity and ennoblement is established, and white racism – exemplified by the prosecutor's final speech, but having many other mani-festations too – is condemned. The critic Armond White has recognized these characteristics in *Sergeant Rutledge*, arguing that the film is 'a cinematic Little Rock' that in relation to other movies 'goes beyond . . . niceties by examining the one issue *The Searchers* avoids: racism as an impulse pumping the heart of American institutions . . . Ford spotlights and casts into relief Americans' professed principles against their daily practices' (White, 2000, p. 33).

If the conscious intention is clear, doubt still remains regarding the unconscious achievement. The allure of, yet fearful repugnance for, the partially known, it can be argued, remains beyond Ford's overt knowledge and control. Probably for all of Ford's career, certainly by 1960, the West of the 1880s was a mythical unknown. So too was black life, for the vast majority of white spectators. These are fantasy areas of life, experienced only through cultural stereotyping. This means that in a black Western the central focus is not ultimately the Negro soldier, for he cannot be the central reality of the picture, existing only as a stereotype. After all, the film actually ends not with the endorsement of Rutledge's good character, but the romantic reconciliation of Lt. Tom Cantrell and Mary Beecher, the two white characters who have throughout believed in the sergeant's innocence. Cantrell's pursuit of truth during the court-martial can also be seen as a courtship of Mary, an affirmation of his own worthiness of character, his own lack of racial prejudice.

One cultural/ideological problem is that most of the black soldiers are undifferentiated, a homogenous group sharing the one common feature of blackness. The ennoblement is achieved through idealization rather than actuality. Rutledge is too perfect, Sergeant Matthew Skidmore is likewise too obedient and easily satisfied. His sentiment expressed to Mary when she (wrongly) denies Cantrell will return Rutledge for trial: 'Soldier can't never think by the heart, ma'am, he gotta think by the book' can be perceived as the way in which a white audience, especially in the tumultuous times of 1960, would want a Negro to think. Skidmore accepts the rules himself, and is content, if not actually happy, to see them accepted by his hierarchical superiors. Sergeant Skidmore is 'at least seventy years old' and has therefore lived most of his life during the period of slavery. He is respected as second only to Rutledge by the other Negro soldiers, so by implication Skidmore's acceptance of subservience as inevitable, and perhaps natural, becomes a general position. The Negroes' nobility is confirmed by its being in accord with the whites' desire to maintain the basic *status quo*: nominal equality tempered by actual inequality.

It is possible to argue that in *Sergeant Rutledge* the black characters are fundamentally, not simply socially, dependent on the whites. Rutledge is intelligent and brave, but it is Lt. Cantrell who brings the patrol through. It is Cantrell who argues the case and uncovers the truth, and it is the white judges – despite their human idiosyncrasies – who ultimately embrace that truth. In Said's argument the white western artist pretends to comprehend, or thinks they do understand, 'other' cultures, but does so only to realign those cultures with white western practices and beliefs.

An awkward aspect of the film is the role of the Apaches. In order for the Negroes to be ennobled, the Indians have to be represented as stereotypical savages: there has to be an alien, it seems. When he gives her a gun to defend herself, Rutledge warns Mary against the marauding Apaches: 'They'll have no mercy on you, lady, they'll have no mercy.' Later he sees them kill Mary's father, which in a rare point-of-view shot the audience witness too, allowing the spectator to authenticate Rutledge's attitude and report. This also helps to validate the idea, although it is not visually depicted, that Chris Hubble has been tortured to death. The film does try to deal with the awkwardness posed by black/red conflict, when as Cpl. Moffit is dying he says to Rutledge: 'We're fools to fight a white man's war.' Rutledge's reply, it can be argued, repositions the polemic within an acceptable framework for a white spectator/director: 'It ain't a white man's war. We're fighting to make us proud.' He appears to be arguing that the white and black man are, then, natural allies against the Indians. If, however, the red and black races are both exploited by whites, Rutledge is suffering from a hegemonic misconception or delusion by identifying black interests with those of white. Rutledge is accepting the right of white characters to control decision-making and therefore the destinies of all races. More specifically, he is telling a predominantly white audience what they want to hear, especially as the words come from the mouth of an honourable Negro.

Thus, the film can be interpreted in diverse ways. While there is perhaps no single and indivisible right way, there may be wrong ways – interpretations that are invalid because they cannot be supported by the text and its period context.

With reference to Ford's last full feature film, 7 Women, the French critic Jean Narboni observed of the director:

> it is less the identification of the enemy that interests him than the emergence
> of an exterior force whatever it is, which, by endangering the uneasy
> co-existence of a disparate group, brings to a head, in an almost beneficial
> way, the crisis of their confrontation.
>
> (Narboni, 1966, p. 24)

Relating this back to Sergeant Rutledge, the red element becomes merely a signifier of the threat that tests the relationship of the black and the white characters. Darby sees a pictorial connection between She Wore a Yellow Ribbon and Sergeant Rutledge that also positions the groups as signifiers, arguing that the movies 'are obviously linked in terms of photographic and compositional style . . . Ford relies on his "iconic" compositions' (Darby, 1996, p. 118). It is this iconic factor that some critics interpret as universalizing, but others perceive as stereotyping, reducing characters to unindividualized types.

It is also possible to discuss Ford's *7 Women* in similar terms. It is set in the literal, geographic Orient as well as exploring the theoretical one with which Orientalists are concerned. From Narboni's point of view there are a number of disparate groups in the movie: North American missionaries, British missionaries of a different religious persuasion (neither are clearly defined theologically), indigenous Chinese and invading Mongols, who obviously represent the 'exterior force'. The situation is complicated, however, by disparities within the groups. As a Chinese woman, for instance, Miss Ling is treated as something of an outsider by almost all the other characters – Americans, British, Mongols, even Chinese. Ultimately, Tunga Khan, the Mongol leader, makes her the servant of his 'woman', and Miss Ling is seen washing the feet of the mistress. It is an action of humiliation, yet she performs it in such a serene manner that it has a biblical resonance. Her black hair and dress, photographed against a light-coloured background, and unusually for Ford from slightly above, because she is kneeling, all give Miss Ling an authority, a stability of character, despite her essential isolation.

Dr Cartwright is an outsider too, for they are linked characters. Ling's isolation within, and from, the main group is partly signified by her place at the dining table, where she sits in the same chair that Cartwright had previously occupied, at the far end from Agatha Andrews, the mission head. Witnessing Ling's degradation, Cartwright asks 'Are you all right?' The latter's reply is typical, as it would also be if coming from the doctor: 'I'm alive.' It is a minimalist, purely pragmatic statement. As part of the subtle thematic relationship of the two women as outsiders, the final view that the other women have of Cartwright is of a figure standing in the main gateway to the compound, wearing Chinese costume and illuminated only by a lantern. Previously she had worn a jacket, shirt and trousers of, for the period, a rather masculine cut. The doctor, as much as the Mongols, is an exterior force within the mission.

As iconic invaders the Mongols are a pure illustration of the threat, menace and horror of the unknown. They are so terrifying that even the Chinese army retreats in the face of their advance. The refugee missionaries, fleeing from the Mongols, describe the atrocities they have committed: 'They killed, mutilated, raped . . . tied the Chinese in bundles of three and threw them into the burning fire – children, old women, they didn't care who. They held them down screaming while they cut off their legs and their arms.' These are indeed inexplicable people, who necessarily have to be reduced to stereotypes in order to be understood and therefore controlled.

When the Mongols enter the mission it is with the due violent mayhem and ritual aggrandisement of Tunga Khan himself. If the power is awful and repellent, it is also awe full and potentially fascinating. Charles Pether has already been murdered and the Chinese driver, Kim, is arbitrarily shot apparently just to intimidate the other characters and create an atmosphere of fear. Lean Warrior, the adjutant, as it were, of the Mongol horde, is energetically ferocious. When Tunga Khan enters, however, he is monumentally static: photographed from a low angle, he sits astride an impressively white horse, his ugly, slightly distorted features suitably enigmatic. It is an awesome power, confirming the earlier reports of atrocities. Yet some of the imprisoned women are fascinated, as though hypnotized by the sheer incomprehensibility of it, by the firing squad and the deadly wrestling match ('They'll kill each other, they're all naked and – yellow . . . what a revolting sight', but spoken gleefully) that ends with Tunga Khan snapping the neck of Lean Warrior.

To some extent the motivation of the characters is stereotyped, simplified for the spectator, who in the end wants the apparently inexplicable explained in terms of ordinary experience. Dr Cartwright's isolation is easily explicable: she is a fugitive from an unhappy love affair. Within the narrative Tunga Khan is driven by a simple lust for power. He is willing to order murder, and to kill with his own hands, but his desire for power also extends to sexuality. In that, it can be argued, he resembles western, or universal, man. It is his narrative weak point, and ultimately leads to his death, when he unwittingly, by attempting to impose his power, hands over control to Cartwright. In murdering Tunga Khan she makes the monster manageable. The Mongol is shown to be like all other men and is therefore controllable. Through the bargain Cartwright struck with Tunga Khan the other women have been freed, and are on their way to safety. Her self-sacrifice, for she faces certain death after murdering the Mongol chief, re-establishes stability in the face of alien threat.

It is impossible to present with any accuracy how Ford felt about the film. It is a strong narrative, and clearly has some parallels with the Western genre, and Ford always denied a conscious ideological intent other than the propagation of tolerance. Yet his presentation of blacks and yellows might seem to raise as many questions as it answers. Although Ford may not have been guilty of overt, or conscious, racism, it could be claimed that he was not entirely innocent of unconscious prejudice. While not deliberately malevolent, he was certainly a product of, and irrevocably trapped within, his time and culture and therefore could not completely avoid its values. White argues that 'Ford is responding to his times as best he can' (White, 2000, p. 39), and maybe that is as much as any artist can achieve.

8 Patriarchy or matriarchy

It is somewhat ironic that Ford, who had never made a 'woman's picture' in the classical Hollywood definition of that genre, should conclude his directorial career with a movie based on so many female characters. At the time, of course, he was unaware that it would be his finale, so the irony is one of fate's making. The timing of the film can be interpreted as having sociocultural significance. 7 Women was made immediately after the first manifestations of contemporary North American feminism, and again it might be argued that the film was an apologetic response to a long neglect. While Ford was generally known as a man's director, a maker of films for mainly male audiences, he did cover a wide range, and a number of his pictures contain extremely interesting women characters.

Forms of feminism had existed in the USA for a very long time, but had perhaps become dormant during the Second World War and its immediate aftermath. To some extent, the contemporary movement stems from Betty Friedan's *The Feminine Mystique*, published in 1963 and running to numerous editions over the following ten or fifteen years. The book starts with a simple assertion that held enormous ramifications:

> *The problem lay buried, unspoken, for many years in the minds of American women. It was a strange stirring, a sense of dissatisfaction, a yearning that women suffered . . . struggled with it alone . . . she was afraid to ask even of herself the silent question – 'Is this all?'*
>
> *(Friedan, 1963, p. 11)*

Friedan goes on to argue that the answer to this question 'may be the next step in human evolution' and that 'the time is at hand when the voices of the feminine mystique can no longer drown out the inner voice that is driving women on to become complete' (ibid., p. 364). The concept of 'feminine mystique' covers the sociocultural constructs and assumptions

7 Women (1966). From left to right: Emma Clark (Sue Lyon), Jane Argent (Mildred Dunnock), Dr Cartwright (Anne Bancroft), Agatha Andrews (Margaret Leighton), Kim (Hans William Lee), Girl (Irene Tsu), Charles Pether (Eddie Albert) and Florrie Pether (Betty Field).

that are placed on women to keep them in subordinate and subservient roles in society at large, and in marriage in particular.

It might be argued that Ford was responding directly to this idea when the emancipated Dr Cartwright winces at hearing the 42-year-old, and first-time pregnant, Florrie Pether, ask 'What's a woman without a child?' Yet in the early morning conversation that Cartwright and Agatha Andrews, the founder and head of the mission, share at the foot of an old tree, the latter confesses in response to the doctor's diagnosis of her emotional state: 'I have to fill my life . . . I've always searched for something that isn't there.' Dr Cartwright replies: 'The mission isn't enough . . . something's missing.' It is a curious conversation, because it opens with Cartwright stating her solution to the problem that they then go on to discuss, which is essentially the question 'Is this all?' The scientific, and apparently liberated, doctor's answer would not please Friedan at all: 'You know, Andrews, you should've married . . . had sons, shared their problems – that's real living.'

Here, Ford appears to be imposing the feminine mystique, and a particularly narrow version of it: a woman's purpose in life is to give birth to sons (coincidentally, Florrie Pether's child is 'a boy'). Lucy Mallory's baby, born during the tortuous journey in *Stagecoach*, is 'a girl', but the really crucial factor about the birth is the way characters' attitudes to it are used as a moral touchstone. Doc Boone is transformed from 'drunken beast' to heroic midwife, and immediately after the birth there are beatific close-ups of Dallas and Ringo as they respond to the new, and vulnerable, life. Those screen images are obviously studio-shot inserts, with anonymous backgrounds and a lot of back-lighting to enhance the divine effect. A little later Ringo's bungling proposal of marriage to the former dance-hall girl (euphemism for whore) is prompted by his recollection of that scene: 'I watched you with that baby . . . you looked, well . . .', and he trails off, inarticulately, but the implied signification is clear – it is her 'natural' attitude to childbirth that redeems any woman. Ford might be seen as having stumbled unintentionally into the patriarchal trap, or, more critically, as actively embracing the values of the patriarch. Again, it becomes a question of the ideological consciousness or unconsciousness of the director. For feminists, it can seem that Ford regards woman as Other – different, alien, threatening, fascinating, unknowable in her own terms and therefore both attractive and dangerous. The fascination, the attraction, and the danger, have to be controlled – and that is achieved by reducing the unknown to terms that are comprehensible.

It was the French theorist Simone de Beauvoir who began to popularize the concept of Otherness in 1949:

> *The category of the* Other *is as primordial as consciousness itself . . . the*
> *expression of a duality – that of the Self and the Other . . . Otherness is a*
> *fundamental category of human thought . . . no group ever sets itself up*
> *as the One without at once setting up the Other over against itself.*
> *(Beauvoir, 1977, pp. 16–17)*

When these assertions are linked to the notion of patriarchy they clearly lead to gender relations. Since 'the two sexes have never shared the world in equality . . . men and women can almost be said to make up two castes' (ibid., p. 20); females are relegated to being the 'Second Sex', and if men are 'the One', women must be that 'Other'.

These are fundamental beliefs informing feminism from the mid-twentieth century on. That is not to say they did not necessarily apply in earlier periods. Miriam Marsh is Davy's childhood sweetheart in *The Iron Horse*, then loses contact with him and becomes engaged to be married to the weak and crooked Peter Jesson, re-meets Davy and ends up ready to marry him. Her life is entirely defined by three men – including her father – and she seems to have very little say in any of it. But she is projected as happy, and quite contentedly accepts these various roles; nor is the film in any way critical of the culture it presents. According to one theoretical interpretation of the movie, the girl is there to be looked at, admired and passed around. It is all natural and beyond question or examination; from a feminist reading it represents a straightforward illustration of the patriarchy's attitude to the Other.

Feminist criticism within film studies became especially prevalent in the 1970s. That stage in its development is to some extent typified by Laura Mulvey's subsequently much anthologized essay, 'Visual pleasure and narrative cinema', in the journal *Screen* (autumn 1975): 'In a world ordered by sexual imbalance, pleasure in looking has been split between active/male and passive/female. The determining male gaze projects its phantasy on to the female figure which is styled accordingly' (Braudy and Cohen, 1999, p. 837). According to this argument the woman functions solely as the object of the male look. This, for a patriarchal audience, confirms woman's inferiority to man. However, since women constitute a large part of the global audience too, male actors might also become the object of a female gaze, albeit in a different psychological/emotional way. In any event, feminist theories, although interesting and useful, are not the only ways in which women characters can, or maybe should, be approached.

Ford did have complex attitudes towards women. He believed in the potential of the continuing beneficial effect of women on men. The eponymous Judge Priest, of the 1934 film, visits the graves of his wife and their children for what Sarris neatly describes as a 'one-sided conversation between the living and the dead' (Sarris, 1998, p. 176). The young Mr Lincoln visits the grave of his sweetheart Ann Rutledge to seek her advice at a critical moment of decision-making. More conventionally, Brittles visits the graves of his wife and children for communion and comfort in *She Wore a Yellow Ribbon*. It could be argued that Ford is simply maintaining the idea of a feminine mystique, the notion that women are essentially unknowable to men because they possess some quasi-supernatural spirituality that puts the female on a different plane of existence. If this were true, it would elevate women, but it also places them outside the social, and can be used, de Beauvoir and Friedan might have reasoned, as a rationale for refusing to allow women full participation in political, economic and cultural life.

One function of Brittles' communions with his dead wife in *She Wore a Yellow Ribbon* is to identify a man who is portrayed otherwise as 'married' solely to the cavalry as having other possibilities too. Brittles was a family man, and after the death of his wife and children the army becomes an alternative commitment. He might be compared with the eponymous Sergeant Rutledge, who appears never to have had any family other than the army. The graveside talks also operate as soliloquies in which Brittles is able to reflect on events and fill in the background details of his character. Sarris has commented: 'with Ford, the emotional emphasis was not so much on the ultimate triumph and vindication of the dead as on the spiritual submission of the living to memory, tradition, and even habit' (Sarris, 1998, p. 176). These are indeed recurring Fordian concerns.

A problem of interpretation arises from the manner in which such scenes are presented. The studio-shot rosy-pinkish twilight of the first cemetery episode in *She Wore a Yellow Ribbon*, for example, accompanied by a sickly string score, emphasizes idealization and falsity of tone. When Olivia arrives at the graveside she initially appears as a shadow on Mary Cutting Brittles' memorial stone, and it is clear that she is destined to become some soldier's young wife, thus continuing the tradition of family service. Depending on how it is viewed, it is possible to see a schism between the intention of the scene and its actual potentially sentimentalizing effect.

There is an inherent difficulty in using an absent character to develop themes, as they can hardly be anything other than passive. Nevertheless, it is true that Ford did use women who were present but not active. *Rio Grande*, for instance, opens with a cavalry troop returning from battle watched by women and children. The linking of these two groups might have an ideological implication: they are the vulnerable who need to be protected. Part of the rationale for the army's presence is to defend women and children from savages – the men *do*, the Others watch and wait patiently. When the soldiers leave for the final battle in *Fort Apache* location long shots of the large cavalry parade are interspersed with five incidents, shot in the studio, of their women, patiently watching. Into a frame of nondescript sky with white cumulous clouds walk three women, who remain standing there. The characters are silent, but a bugle call can be heard off screen. As the soldiers begin to leave, singing in chorus, we cut to a group of three women in close-up; later, two older women appear in mid-shot partly against a door and window, their faces registering pain and anxiety. The final two scenes depict a group of women on a veranda. Apart from the shot of the two older women, all the groupings are photographed from a low angle, looking down. They are suffering on behalf of their menfolk, their anxiety possibly more acute, since they can only stand and wait. The effect is to make them statuesque, gnostic. However, this could be interpreted as removing them from real experience, the reality of what it is to be a woman in such a patriarchal society. According to such an interpretation, they fulfil that centuries-old stereotype of woman Shakespeare celebrated: 'like Patience on a monument' (*Twelfth Night*, II, iv, 115).

When women do become active they can be dangerous, or wrong-headed. When Mrs Collingwood receives the news of her husband's transfer, which would save him from going into the final – and for him fatal – battle, the other women urge her to send after the troop and bring him back. But she decides not to, on the grounds that Maj. Collingwood is 'no coward'. Thus, she creates the circumstances of her husband's death, albeit unintentionally. On another level, in *She Wore a Yellow Ribbon* Olivia is a typical coquette, playing off the young lieutenants Cohill and Pennell against one another with such expertise as to bring them to the verge of an actual fist-fight. While her behaviour might be excused as immature thoughtlessness, occasionally Ford's women characters appear to be positively malevolent. There are two classic examples of this: Lora Nash in the 1932 *Flesh* manipulates the hapless Polokai into marriage just so that she can exploit him for the benefit of her feckless lover; Freda helps to entrap Ole Olsen into the attempted shanghai plot in *The Long Voyage Home*. Ultimately, however, they regret their actions. With such characters, it seems, Ford places a two-way bet – getting both the evil of the temptress, but also the purification of redemption.

Nevertheless, Ford could, and did, present extremely active females. Mary Beecher kills an Apache attacker with the revolver Sergeant Rutledge gives her for self-defence. And as early as 1924 the saloon girls in *The Iron Horse* joined in the defence of the railroad unit when the Indians attacked, shooting rifles with the best of the men. Less dramatically, but just as effectively, Mary Kate contests the question of sovereignty in their relationship with Sean Thornton in *The Quiet Man*. Her line 'They'll be no dinner tonight' is redolent with a menace that goes beyond the mere matter of 'dinner' and 'tonight'. Somewhat similarly, Amelia Sarah Dedham stands up to Donovan in *Donovan's Reef*, demanding respect from a character who through most of the movie is an ingrained male supremacist. In *7 Women* Cartwright virtually takes control of the mission, defeating the cholera epidemic, delivering the baby successfully in the most appalling circumstances, confronting the invading Mongols, winning freedom for the other women and finally killing Tunga Khan.

Cartwright, however, is an aberration, and provides a role model for no one. The French theorist Jean-Louis Comolli has observed:

> the 'super-hero', Dr Cartwright . . . is displaced at least three times: as a woman in a man's profession, as an American on the Chinese border, as an atheist in a religious community and, by extension a traitor to her own worlds and its morals, without counting her irony which makes her completely unsentimental.
>
> (Comolli, 1966, p. 17)

This 'super-hero' is clearly a liberated woman, who claims to be as a doctor 'better than a man'. But there are ways in which she is more masculine than female, given the period setting of 1935: she smokes cigarettes almost constantly, gets drunk on whiskey and her dress and behaviour signify maleness. She enters the mission riding a mule and wearing trousers, and does not appear in a conventional western female dress throughout the film. In 1949, almost midway between the making of the picture and its setting (1965 and 1935 respectively), de Beauvoir had written 'that humanity is divided into two classes of individuals whose clothes, faces, bodies, smiles, gaits, interests, and occupations are manifestly different' (Beauvoir, 1977, pp. 14–15). Cartwright offends against several of these categorizations, including that of gait, for she often swaggers, and her costume allows her to stride and run in a way that the other women cannot.

Ultimately, though, the doctor is not a pointer to the future, for she is literally self-destructive. Her death can be seen as an act of self-sacrifice, for by killing Tunga Khan she sentences herself to death, but in the process gains the freedom of the other women. It is not, however, that straightforward. What Comolli describes as 'her irony' can also be interpreted as a posture of self-defence against a world, a fate, that has let her down. The smoking and drinking, her very presence in that unlikely place, are all signifiers that she is heading for self-destruction from the very moment of her first appearance in the movie.

In addition to Cartwright's very real and evident care for the sick, she has a saving grace too, a Fordian redemptive feature, in her relationship with Emma Clark. Andrews is drawn to the youngest member of the mission too, but in a way that suggests a repressed lesbian attraction. Andrews touches Emma's shoulder when the latter is washing, wearing only her underclothes, and later places her hand on Emma's when they are sitting together under the tree in the centre of the compound. These are not maternal moments. Andrews seems to want to dominate the younger woman. Cartwright, on the other hand, consistently advises Emma to get out of the mission, to find another life in the larger world.

It is ironic that Cartwright's suggestion to Andrews that she should have been a mother takes place under the tree where Andrews has recently touched Emma's hand, perhaps with a desire she quickly covers by withdrawal, for it is Cartwright herself who behaves most like a mother to the young woman. The best of Fordian women, those he appears to approve of most, are mothers, the maternal instinct itself often being redemptive in the films.

Ma Joad in *The Grapes of Wrath* provides an illustration. It is she who struggles to hold the family together against overwhelming and increasing odds. Pa Joad admits: 'You the one that keeps us goin', Ma. I ain't no good no more.' The critic Tom Stempel, commenting on scenarist Johnson's methods, shrewdly points out:

The first line of that speech . . . is not from the novel, although the rest of the speech is. By adding that line, Johnson has done two things. He has given the dramatic motivation for Ma's speeches that follow, and he has expressed his own view of the world in which the man should be the strong, active member of the family and the wife the helpmate.

(Stempel, 1980, p. 82)

This is a timely reminder that films are collaborative ventures, but in this case there is no reason to think that Ford would have disagreed with any of the sentiments.

Most of Ma's speeches are taken from the novel, although their order is changed in the movie. She expresses a Fordian ideal, albeit one not invariably realized:

'A woman can change better'n a man. A man lives, sorta – well, in jerks. Baby born, or somebody dies, that's a jerk . . . with a woman it's all in one flow like a stream – little eddies, little waterfalls, but the river it goes right on. A woman looks at it that way.'

It is the continuity that is crucial, and which is maintained by mothers in particular. It is possible to argue that limiting women to motherhood is a patriarchal method of restricting their horizons. Although speaking Steinbeck's words, through Johnson's reordering of them and Ford's direction, Ma links women to oppressed humanity in general: 'Rich fellas come up, they die – their kids ain't no good, an' they die out – but we keep a-comin'. We're the people that live. They can't wipe us out, they can't lick us. We'll go on for ever . . . we're the people.' These words are given emphasis by being the last speeches in the movie. In directing them, Ford gives great prominence to Ma Joad in a long take in which she and Pa are photographed through the windscreen of their truck, with unnaturally bright lighting, perhaps connoting a mood of hope after all the misfortunes. Ma is positioned slightly nearer the camera than Pa, so that although they share the frame, she is the larger, more powerful and impressive figure. Motherhood is presented as indomitable, carrying the continuity from past, through present to future.

Beth Morgan, the central mother figure in *How Green Was My Valley*, is physically quite like Ma Joad. Probably in their forties or fifties, both women are short, and stocky, a little plump, but healthily so, with hair pulled back tight and neat. (The word that summarizes both characters' physical attributes is matronly.) Both are matriarchs. But perhaps it is only a patriarch's view of matriarchy. The women run the families, while the men have the overt, superficial power, but ultimately it is the mothers/

wives who keep the show together. Ma Joad and Mrs Morgan both have strapping sons whom they keep in order as best they can in hostile circumstances. The Joad family is broken up by their economic situation, and the Morgans suffer the same fate. Beth attempts to mediate during family arguments, and to maintain harmony and solidarity – and to some extent she succeeds. Mrs Morgan's failures are caused by a miners' strike, by deteriorating economic circumstances that send two of her sons to America in search of a better life and ultimately by a death in a pit accident. But the indomitable will remains.

The narrative voice-over analyses family life: 'If my father was the head of the house, my mother was its heart.' She was the engine too: 'My mother was always on the run. Always the last to start the dinner, always the first to finish.' Beth Morgan was also a tigress in defence of her family. When her husband is threatened with physical violence for not joining a colliers' strike, she addresses a meeting of strikers that is being held in a blizzard, promising: 'If any harm comes to my Gwilym I'll find out the men and I will kill them, with my two hands.' Dressed in black and resembling an avenging angel of the Old Testament, she is framed from a low angle against falling snow and the sound of a howling wind. Yet after she has recovered from a serious illness the men of the village congregate outside the Morgans' house to sing in praise; then all Beth can say is 'Come and eat, everyone.' Beth Morgan embodies the very best elements of Fordian motherhood: emotional strength, energy, fierce loyalty and generosity of both spirit and table.

Ford admired and respected such women, but they might be seen, too, as examples of the oppression of patriarchy, trapping women into traditional matriarchal roles that are defined by men, for men's benefit, while pretending it is for the woman's good. Friedan wrote of this entrapment:

> Experts told them [young women] how to catch a man and keep him, how to breastfeed children . . . how to cope with sibling rivalry and adolescent rebellion . . . how to dress, look, and act . . . They were taught to pity the neurotic . . . unhappy women who wanted to be poets or physicists or presidents.
>
> (Friedan, 1963, p. 11)

It is interesting that while Hallie, in The Man Who Shot Liberty Valance, gained prosperity and social advantages through being educated by, and marrying, Ransom Stoddard, ultimately there is the sense of a lost life. It is not suggested that Ransom was in any way a bad husband, or that her life as a senator's wife was wasted, but in making that choice she forwent the pleasures of a more ordinary, common life with Tom Doniphon, a man who was so dedicated to her happiness that he was literally willing to kill for it. The sterility of Hallie's life is thematically signified partly by the lack of a Stoddard family.

On the whole Ford eschewed the use of purely 'sex object' actresses. The younger women characters were always presented as physically attractive within the conventions of the times. As illustrations, Jean Arthur in *The Whole Town's Talking* (1935), Katharine Hepburn in *Mary of Scotland* (1936), Maureen O'Hara in *The Quiet Man* and other movies were all exceptionally photogenic. They were, nevertheless, not pin-ups. Only Dorothy Lamour (*The Hurricane* (1937)) really falls into that category. For *7 Women* Ford had Sue Lyon foisted on him, partly because she was big box office after playing Lolita in Stanley Kubrick's 1962 film of Nabokov's novel. Lyon was the highest paid member of the cast of *7 Women*, but she played against type as a teacher in a religious community. Ford used the blondness and youth that often signifies sexuality as a signifier instead of innocence and purity. Carroll Baker illustrates a similar case in *Cheyenne Autumn*. The roles and scenario partly determine character, of course, but Ford emphasized the qualities of innocence and purity, and diminished any possible lusty sexuality, by the manner in which he shot the characters. They are, for instance, always associated with light, often bright outdoor sunlight, rather than dimly lit interiors that might suggest carnal activity. Lusty sexuality in women was something Ford treated very tentatively, avoiding it all together if possible. Even the many prostitutes in his pictures are merely doing a job.

Unusually, for Hollywood society, Ford had only one wife, to whom he was married for over fifty years. It is suspected, however, that he did indulge in some extramarital liaisons. His relationship with Katharine Hepburn is steeped in mystery, with some contemporaries convinced that there was a sexual affair, and others claiming it was purely platonic. Later, there were similar rumours involving Maureen O'Hara. Nothing has ever been substantiated in those cases, but during his 1958 trip to Korea Ford, according to the scrupulous biographer Eyman, engaged in a relationship with the Korean actress Heran Moon. Gallagher has written of Ford's marriage and dalliances: 'He was permitted his extramarital affairs, of which there were not a few ... conducted with extreme circumspection' (Gallagher, 1986, p. 380). Perhaps Ford's main difficulty with women was one shared by other men – that mothers must be pure, but in order to become one it is necessary to have carnal knowledge. For such men, too much sexual desire in a woman appears to go beyond the biological, and family, need. Mothers need to be, in many of Ford's movies, paragons of virtue.

Ford's belief in the importance of paragon mothers might be attributed in part to his own upbringing as the youngest son in a very large Catholic family. Throughout his life he claimed to be a practising Catholic, and the enthusiastic Sarris was so irritated by one of Ford's pictures he wrote:

> *the glowingly pro-Catholic propaganda in* The Fugitive *seemed very naïve indeed. Even in 1947, it seemed unfair to stack the deck for the Catholic Church in any Latin American setting, however allegorical. What was paradoxical in the Greene novel became polemical in the Ford film, and what was dialectical became dogmatic.*
>
> (Sarris, 1998, p. 206)

In 1947 the Roman Catholic Church was fighting a battle on at least two fronts: the conflict against God-less Communism at the beginning of the cold war; and the struggle to be at the centre of democratic political life having been tainted with fascist collaboration. Ford could hardly have been unaware of these factors at the time, and it is not impossible that he saw *The Fugitive*, as Sarris implies, in a propagandist light.

In more general terms the Catholic Church had always placed a high priority on the veneration of the Virgin Mary as the Mother of the Son of God. Motherhood was taken extremely seriously by the Vatican. An illustration of this is provided by an address made by Pope Pius XII in 1951 praising and demanding: 'An eager acceptance of the vocation of mother-hood! . . . a sincere acceptance of the duties of motherhood. On this condition, the woman follows the path traced by the Creator to the end He has appointed for the creature' (Pope Pius XII, 1960, pp. 13–14). There is no reason at all why Ford should have been familiar with this speech in particular, but as a lifelong Catholic he would have been imbued with its sentiments, which are simply being stated here as an expression of traditional belief.

Robert Parrish, who worked with Ford as an editor on several films, including *The Battle of Midway*, reported that the director said of the picture, 'It's for the mothers of America' (Parrish, 1976, p. 145). Clearly, mother-hood did mean something very special to Ford, and affected the way he perceived, and his attitude towards, women in general. In his eyes, they had a tremendous potential for good, or a great capacity to ruin a man. For example, in *Rio Grande*, when Mrs Yorke, tries to buy her son out of the army on the grounds that she knows what is best for him, she is in danger of destroying the boy she sincerely loves. Mothers can keep families together, but also must know when to let go.

Ford had an unerring ear for sententiousness, which is brought out strongly in *Young Mr Lincoln*. John Felder, the prosecutor in the Clay brothers' trial, makes a speech dubiously claiming the good character of the loutish murder victim, Scrub White: 'peace loving . . . a man, an American, in whose veins flowed the blood of pioneers, who braved the wilderness to make this great State what it is', and so on in rhetorical eulogy. This is undermined visually and aurally by a cutaway to Judge Bell asleep and snoring heavily.

When, later, Lincoln eulogizes the brothers' mother, Mrs Abigail Clay, there is no such cinematic subversion. In a tense and attentive courtroom Lincoln dominates the frame, mainly with Abigail to one side of it on the witness stand and the judge in the background. The filmic presentation underlines the seriousness of the speech: Mrs Clay 'can't even write her own name – yet has she no feelings, no *heart*?' Lincoln stresses that last word to Judge Bell, and the camera. It emphasizes the ordinariness of the specific woman, the commonality of the particular – the film is set in the 1830s but the metaphoric point remains – that the picture is concerned with at this juncture. Flanked by Abigail on screen, Lincoln extends the generalization, describing how he has known many such women: 'working in the fields, kitchens, hovering over some sick and helpless child – women who say little, but do much, who ask for nothing but give all'. Ford is clearly endorsing the value of self-sacrifice, which he sees as one of the crucial virtues of good motherhood.

It might also be argued that Ford eulogized the family in theory because he appears to have been such a poor family man himself in practice. A recurring drunk and an alleged fornicator, he was a father who apparently so tyrannized his two children that both grew up very unhappily with deep-seated neuroses. The ideal family, centring on the ideal mother, could therefore act as a fantasy substitute for the inadequacies of Ford's own life.

As always, there are other ways of interpreting the films. It may be that Friedan, de Beauvoir, Mulvey and many other theorists would see Ford's representation as imposing the notion of feminine mystique on women in order to keep them in their place – the kitchen and the bedroom. While this is undoubtedly a valid point, any single theoretical approach to any text should not exclude the possibility of other interpretations. The theorist Frederic Jameson defined the text, any film in this case, as a 'free floating object' (Jameson, 1981, p. 70). One way of understanding this concept is not that a movie can have absolutely any interpretation placed on it, but that more than one valid reading might be possible. Ford's film women are diverse, living in, and shifting between, both patriarchal and matriarchal worlds depending on the context at the moment.

Further reading

Anderson, L. (1999) *About John Ford* (Plexus, London).

An idiosyncratic approach to the films, but nevertheless a valuable insight into a director's view of Ford's work that also contains many personal observations on Ford's character too, along with revealing interviews with some of Ford's collaborators, especially writers and actors.

Baxter, J. (1971) *The Cinema of John Ford* (Tantivy Press, London).

An enthusiastic approach to the films, which perhaps lacks the critical edge on occasions; although John Baxter's dismissal of *Cheyenne Autumn* and *7 Women* with the judgement that *Donovan's Reef* was 'Ford's last important film' (p. 172) displays a cavalier attitude that is certainly not blunt. The book also suffers from a predominantly chronological structure that discourages a linking of themes across time. Nevertheless, it contains many perceptive analytical comments that remain valid.

Bogdanovich, P. (1978) *John Ford* (University of California Press, London).

Based on interviews with Ford, some more constructive than others, Bogdanovich brings a critical enthusiasm to bear on the subject, both as a person and a director. What Ford manages to avoid saying is sometimes as revealing as his statements.

Braudy, L. and Cohen, M. (eds) (1999) *Film Theory and Criticism: Introductory Readings*, fifth edition (Oxford University Press, Oxford).

The very fact that the book is now in its fifth, and extended, edition speaks for itself. The whole range of film studies, both in terms of subject matter and historical perspective, is covered in the 861 pages that now include a useful index. Previous editions appeared under the joint editorship of Gerald Mast, Marshall Cohen and Leo Braudy.

Browne, N. (ed.) (1990) *Cahiers du Cinéma*, vol. 3 (Routledge, London).

For a general summary of the usefulness, and importance, of the translations from this journal, see Hillier below. This volume covers the period from 1969 to 1972, continuing where Volume 2 ends.

Buscombe, E. (1992) *Stagecoach* (British Film Institute, London).

A thorough analysis of the film and its production context that provides a lot of detail concerning the whole process from conception to reviews and criticism.

Buscombe, E. (2000) *The Searchers* (British Film Institute, London).

Another title in the British Film Institute's valuable series, following the standard format.

Carey, H. Jr (1994) *Company of Heroes: My Life as an Actor in the John Ford Stock Company* (Scarecrow Press, London).

Known as Dobe, because of the colour of his hair, the author was the son of the great silent star Harry Carey and the actress Olive Carey, and a godson of Ford. Consequently, it is in part an intimate account of working with the director, and of Ford in private life; but because of the personal involvement, it is a partial view too.

Caughie, J. (ed.) (1999) *Theories of Authorship* (Routledge, London).

An invaluable anthology of pieces on the vexed issue of auteurism. Originally published in 1981, and divided into three sections, the book comprehensively covers the main theoretical positions up to that time. These positions have not changed essentially, and this reprint has been long overdue. For a 1990s extension of the theories, see Collins, et al. (1993), and Corrigan (1991) in the Bibliography.

Darby, W. (1996) *John Ford's Westerns: A Thematic Analysis, with a Filmography* (McFarland and Company, Jefferson, NC).

William Darby mainly considers films in pairs, working through ideas of contrasts. The concept is useful for analysis, and the filmography provides a good practical tool for detailed research. The book's only limitation is implied in its title, as it has to ignore two-thirds of Ford's work that falls outside the genre. Otherwise it is an enjoyable and stimulating read.

Eyman, S. (1999) *Print the Legend: The Life and Times of John Ford* (Simon and Schuster, New York).

Comprehensive and well written, this by far the best full critical biography of Ford. Eyman is an enthusiast who is nonetheless prepared to criticize the movies he considers Ford's less successful work. The author quotes from documents not previously published, and juxtaposes information in new and intriguing ways.

Ford, D. (1998) *Pappy: The Life of John Ford* (Da Capo, New York).

Dan Ford is a son of Patrick Ford, and John Ford's grandson. He served with some distinction in Vietnam, a fact that gave much pleasure to his grandfather, and later became a Hollywood producer. It is an interesting book, though, as might be expected in the circumstances, needs to be read with a critically open mind.

Gallagher, T. (1986) *John Ford: The Man and His Films* (University of California Press, Berkeley).

Until Eyman's more recent book (see above), this was undoubtedly the best full critical biography on Ford. It still has the most comprehensive filmography available. In so far as this extremely valuable book has limitations, it is in the author's overenthusiasm for some of the director's minor movies, and the use of unnecessary comparisons with other directors, such as Hitchcock and Hawkes, to demonstrate Ford's superiority as a film-maker.

Grant, B.K. (ed.) (1997) *Film Genre Reader II*, second edition (University of Texas Press, Austin).

An extremely comprehensive anthology of 581 pages covering many aspects of the difficult subject of genre. The book is divided into two sections. Almost a third is devoted to pure genre theory, and includes essays by such specialists as Neale, Altman and Tudor, as well as Grant himself. The second section presents specific studies, such as pieces by Pye and Gallagher on diverse aspects of the Western.

Hillier, J. (ed.) (1996) *Cahiers du Cinéma*, vol. 1 (Routledge, London).
Hillier, J. (ed.) (1996) *Cahiers du Cinéma*, vol. 2 (Routledge, London).

An excellently selected compilation of pieces from the most influential journal in continuous publication during the period covered by these two volumes collectively, the early 1950s to the political watershed year of 1968. Various translators are used to transform the French texts into very readable English.

Lyons, R. (ed.) (1990) *My Darling Clementine: John Ford, Director* (Rutgers University Press, New Brunswick, NJ).

A useful anthological approach to the title film, covering a wide range of views, opinions and material.

McBride, J. (2000) *Searching for John Ford* (London, Faber).

Another comprehensive critical biography from an established critic. Among other approaches, McBride traces possible biographical influences in the films. He argues that Ford was a spy for the US navy before Pearl Harbor, using his own yacht, the *Araner*, to cruise the Pacific Ocean picking up information about Japanese shipping. While there has been a long-standing rumour to this effect, to which Ford did not too strenuously object, no conclusive proof has been presented.

McBride J. and Wilmington, M. (1988) *John Ford* (Da Capo, New York).

Although a fine scholarly work with some interesting interview material, it has been somewhat superseded by McBride's more recent biography. Nevertheless, fine critical points emerge from the thematic structure of the book: 'The Noble Outlaw', 'Men at War', etc.

Nichols, B. (ed.) (1976) *Movies and Methods*, vol. 1 (University of California Press, Berkeley).
Nichols, B. (ed.) (1985) *Movies and Methods*, vol. 2 (University of California Press, Berkeley).

In these two books Bill Nichols has pulled together an enormous range of essays, presenting both purely theoretical debates and incisive illustrations of how those theories are put into practice. Auteurism, ideology, genre and mise-en-scène are all aspects of film studies that are covered by an international array of theorists and critics.

Place, J.A. (1974) *The Western Films of John Ford* (Citadel, New York).
Place, J.A. (1981) *The Non-Western Films of John Ford* (Citadel, New York).

The films are considered in discrete chapters, and although the analysis is interesting, and sometimes very perceptive indeed, the books as a whole seem to lack a central argument or coherence. Anyone who reads Anderson (1999) should also read Janey Place, if only to see what really makes him so angry.

Sarris, A. (1976) *The John Ford Movie Mystery* (Secker and Warburg, London).

Andrew Sarris was one of the first US theorists to champion Ford's work. The insights are often penetrating, and despite his enthusiasm Sarris is also willing to identify those pictures that he thinks are inferior to the major output. The main limitation of an exceedingly useful and interesting book is that the approach is largely chronological, to the detriment of the movies' thematic coherence.

Wollen, P. (1998) *Signs and Meaning in the Cinema*, third edition, revised and enlarged (British Film Institute, London).

This was a seminal work when the original version was published in 1969, adding new dimensions to semiological approaches to film studies. Since then the book has been revised and extended to take into account other theoretical developments. It has, rightly, become a standard work in its field, and although parts of it have been much anthologized, the whole remains a stimulating and rewarding read.

Bibliography

Astor, M. (1973) *A Life on Film* (W.H. Allen, London)

Balio, T. (ed.) (1985) *The American Film Industry*, revised edition (University of Wisconsin Press, Madison)

Beauvoir, S. de (1977) *The Second Sex*, translated by Richard Howard (Penguin, Harmondsworth)

Bordwell, D., Staiger, J. and Thompson, K. (1985) *The Classical Hollywood Cinema: Film Style and Mode of Production to 1960* (Routledge, London)

Branigan, E. (1998) *Narrative Comprehension and Film* (Routledge, London)

Braudy, L. (1999) 'Genre: the conventions of connection', in Braudy, L. and Cohen, M. (eds) *Film Theory and Criticism: Introductory Readings*, fifth edition (Oxford University Press, Oxford) pp. 613–29

Buckland, W. (1998) *Film Studies* (Hodder and Stoughton, London)

Buscombe, E. (1999) 'Ideas of authorship', in Caughie, J. (ed.) *Theories of Authorship* (Routledge, London) pp. 22–34

Butler, J.G. (1991) *Star Texts: Image and Performance in Film and Television* (Wayne State University Press, Detroit)

Cahiers du Cinéma (1976) 'John Ford's *Young Mr Lincoln*', in Nichols, B. (ed.) *Movies and Methods*, vol. 1 (University of California Press, Berkeley) pp. 493–528

Carnes, M.C. (ed.) (1996) *Past Imperfect: History According to the Movies* (Cassell, London)

Chafe, W.H. (1986) *The Unfinished Journey: America Since World War II* (Oxford University Press, Oxford)

Christie, I. (1998) 'Formalism and neo-formalism', in Hill, J. and Gibson, P.C. (eds) *The Oxford Guide to Film Studies* (Oxford University Press, Oxford) pp. 58–64

Collins, J., Radner, H. and Collins, A.P. (eds) (1993) *Film Theory Goes to the Movies* (Routledge, New York)

Comolli, J.-L. (1966) 'Dé-composition', *Cahiers du Cinéma* **182**(9): 16–20

Corrigan, T. (1991) *Cinema Without Walls* (Routledge, London)

Davies, P. and Neve, B. (eds) (1981) *Cinema, Politics and Society in America* (Manchester University Press, Manchester)

Bibliography

Dewey, D. (1998) *James Stewart: A Biography* (Warner Books, London)

Everson, W.K. (1978) *American Silent Film* (Oxford University Press, New York)

Eyman, S. (1987) *Five American Cinematographers* (Scarecrow Press, London)

Friedan, B. (1963) *The Feminine Mystique* (Dell Publishing, New York)

Frough, W. (1972) *The Screenwriter Looks at the Screenwriter* (Macmillan, New York)

Grant, B.K. (1997) 'Experience and meaning in genre films', in Grant, B.K. (ed.) *Film Genre Reader II*, second edition (University of Texas Press, Austin) pp. 114–28

Henderson, B. (1985) '*The Searchers*: an American dilemma', in Nichols, B. (ed.) *Movies and Methods*, vol. 2 (University of California Press, Berkeley) pp. 429–49

Hill, J. and Gibson, P.C. (eds) (1998) *The Oxford Guide to Film Studies* (Oxford University Press, Oxford)

Huettig, M.D. (1985) 'Economic control of the motion picture industry', in Balio, T. (ed.) *The American Film Industry*, revised edition (University of Wisconsin Press, Madison) pp. 285–310

Jameson, F. (1981) *The Political Unconscious: Narrative as a Socially Symbolic Act* (Methuen, London)

Jones, M.A. (1991) *The Limits of Liberty* (Oxford University Press, Oxford)

Kitses, J. (1969) *Horizons West* (Thames and Hudson, London)

Kochberg, S. (1996) 'Cinema as institution', in Nelmes, J. (ed.) *An Introduction to Film Studies* (Routledge, London) pp. 7–59

Lapsley, R. and Westlake, M. (1988) *Film Theory: An Introduction* (Manchester University Press, Manchester)

McCabe, J. (1998) *Cagney* (Aurum Press, London)

Maltby, R. (1981) 'The political economy of Hollywood: the studio system', in Davies, P. and Neve, B. (eds) *Cinema, Politics and Society in America* (Manchester University Press, Manchester) pp. 42–58

Maltby, R. (1999) *Hollywood Cinema: An Introduction* (Blackwell, Oxford)

Marriage and the Moral Law: Addresses of Pope Pius XII (1960), revised edition (Catholic Truth Society, London)

Mulvey, L. (1999) 'Visual pleasure and narrative cinema', in Braudy, L. and Cohen, M. (eds) *Film Theory and Criticism: Introductory Readings*, fifth edition (Oxford University Press, Oxford) pp. 833–44

Narboni, J. (1966) 'La preuve par huit,' *Cahiers du Cinéma* **182**(9): pp. 20–24

Neale, S. (1997) 'Questions of genre', in Grant, B.K. (ed.) *Film Genre Reader II*, second edition (University of Texas Press, Austin) pp. 159–83

Neely, M.E. Jr (1996) 'The young Lincoln', in Carnes, M.C. (ed.) *Past Imperfect: History According to the Movies* (Cassell, London) pp. 124–7

Nelmes, J. (ed.) (1996) *An Introduction to Film Studies* (Routledge, London)

Oates, S.B. (1994) *Let the Trumpet Sound: A Life of Martin Luther King, Jr* (Payback Press, Edinburgh)

Parrish, R. (1976) *Growing Up in Hollywood* (Bodley Head, London)

Patterson, J.T. (1994) *America in the Twentieth Century: A History*, fourth edition (HBJ, London)

Pearce, J. (1981) *Under the Eagle* (Latin American Bureau, London)

Phillips, P. (1996) 'Genre, star and auteur: an approach to Hollywood cinema', in Nelmes, J. (ed.) *An Introduction to Film Studies* (Routledge, London) pp. 121–63

Pope Pius XII see *Marriage and the Moral Law*

Richie, D. (1984) *The Films of Akira Kurosawa* (University of California Press, Berkeley)

Roberts, R. and Olson, J.S. (1995) *John Wayne: American* (Free Press, New York)

Robinson, D. (1968) *Hollywood in the Twenties* (Tantivy Press, London)

Rollins, P.C. (ed.) (1983) *Hollywood as Historian* (University Press of Kentucky, Lexington)

Rosenbaum, J. (ed.) (1993) *This Is Orson Welles* (HarperCollins, London)

Ryall, T. (1998) 'Genre and Hollywood', in Hill, J. and Gibson, P.C. (eds) *The Oxford Guide to Film Studies* (Oxford University Press, Oxford) pp. 327–38

Said, E.W. (1995) *Orientalism* (Penguin, Harmondsworth)

Sarris, A. (1998) *'You Ain't Heard Nothin' Yet': The American Talking Film: History and Memory, 1927–1949* (Oxford University Press, Oxford)

Sarris, A. (1999) 'Notes on the auteur theory in 1962', in Braudy, L. and Cohen, M. (eds) *Film Theory and Criticism: Introductory Readings*, fifth edition (Oxford University Press, Oxford) pp. 515–18

Schatz, T. (1981) *Hollywood Genres: Formulas, Filmmaking, and the Studio System* (Temple University Press, Philadelphia)

Scorsese, M. and Wilson, M.H. (1997) *A Personal Journey with Martin Scorsese Through American Movies* (Faber, London)

Shakespeare, W. (1975) *Twelfth Night* (Methuen, London)

Sinclair, A. (1979) *John Ford* (Dial, New York)

Sobchack, T. and Sobchack, V.C. (eds) (1987) *An Introduction to Film Studies*, second edition (Scott, Foresman and Company, Glenview, IL)

Sobchack, V. (1983) *'The Grapes of Wrath* (1940): 'thematic emphasis through visual style', in Rollins, P.C. (ed.) *Hollywood as Historian* (University Press of Kentucky, Lexington) pp. 68–87

Sontag, S. (ed.) (1983) *Barthes: Selected Writings* (Fontana/Collins, London)

Stempel, T. (1980) *Screenwriter Nunnally Johnson* (A.S. Barnes, New York)

Tavernier, B. (1994) 'Notes of a Press Attache', *Film Comment*, **30**(4): p. 38

Thompson, K. and Bordwell, D. (1994) *Film History: An Introduction* (McGraw-Hill, New York)

Tudor, A. (1974) *Theories of Film* (Secker and Warburg, London)

Warshow, R. (1999) 'Movie chronicle: The Westerner', in Braudy, L. and Cohen, M. (eds) *Film Theory and Criticism: Introductory Readings*, fifth edition (Oxford University Press, Oxford) pp. 654–67

White, A. (2000), 'Stepping forward looking back', *Film Comment*, **36**(2): pp. 33–9

Williams, L. (1999) 'Film bodies: gender, genre, and excess', in Braudy, L. and Cohen, M. (eds) *Film Theory and Criticism: Introductory Readings*, fifth edition (Oxford University Press, Oxford) pp. 701–15

Wills, G. (1999) *John Wayne: The Politics of Celebrity* (Faber, London)

Wood, R. (1999) 'Ideology, genre, auteur', in Braudy, L. and Cohen, M. (eds) *Film Theory and Criticism: Introductory Readings*, fifth edition (Oxford University Press, Oxford) pp. 668–78

Index